T0125715

THOUSAND$ PER MINUTE

"How to sell is one thing. How to sell well is another. How to sell well at a distance via a camera lens is a completely unique specialist skill, but it's something that Cory is a master at! There are few people in the world I would trust to hone my sales message on-screen. With his record and this book, Cory has earned a place on that list. The next time you sell on TV or online video, make sure Cory's with you!"

—**James Lavers**, On-camera sales trainer,
specialist in video persuasion, "video psychologist"

"Many claim to know how to sell, but cannot substantiate that claim with the level of insight Cory wields. In his own entertaining way, Cory boldly goes where few have been willing to. He lays out the secret sauce behind real TV and video sales success. Every person looking to sell a product in front of a camera should read this book."

—**Kevin Harrington**, Infomercial mogul
and investor from the hit TV show *Shark Tank*

"Cory's experience behind and in front of the camera adds a unique and invaluable insight into what it takes to achieve success in the arena of product sales on tv and using video. His skills are valuable to inventors, marketers, tv hosts and presenters, sales rep, product developers and so many more. His perspective and experience are invaluable. This book is one of the most insightful and helpful tools to selling on camera that I have ever seen. Cory's depth of understanding and practical, yet entertaining way of sharing his knowledge is unparalleled. As someone who has also spent years in this field of pitching products, I give this book my highest endorsement and only wish I had access to this info when I was starting out!"

—**Forbes Riley**, *The 2 Billion Dollar Host /*
TV Health & Fitness Celebrity

THOUSAND$
PER
MINUTE

The Art of Pitching Products
on Internet, Video and Television

Cory Bergeron

NEW YORK

THOUSAND$ PER MINUTE

The Art of Pitching Products on Internet, Video and Television

Published in New York, New York, by Morgan James Publishing. Morgan James and The Entrepreneurial Publisher are trademarks of Morgan James, LLC.
www.MorganJamesPublishing.com

The Morgan James Speakers Group can bring authors to your live event. For more information or to book an event visit The Morgan James Speakers Group at
www.TheMorganJamesSpeakersGroup.com.

Mr. Mom. Words and Music by Richie McDonald, Ronald Harbin and Don Mr. Mom written by Ron Harbin, Richie McDonald, & Don Pfrimmer. © 2004 Sony/ATV Music Publishing LLC. All rights on behalf of Sony/ATV Music Publishing LLCadministered by Sony/ATV Music. Publishing LLC, 8 Music Square West, Nashville, TN 37203. All rights reserved. Used by permission. Words and music by Richie McDonald, Ronald Harbin and Don Pfrimmer. © 2004 Sony/ATV Songs LLC, Harbinism.com Music, Don Pfrimmer Music, Sassy Mule Music, Super ID Music and Top Mule Music. All rights on behalf of Sony/ATV Songs LLC administered by Sony/ATV Music Publishing LLC, 424 Church Street, Suite 1200, Nashville, TN 37219. All rights on behalf of Harbinism.com Music administered by BMG Rights Management (US) LLC. All rights on behalf of Don Pfrimmer Music administered by Wixen Music Publishing Inc. All rights on behalf of Sassy Mule Music, Super ID Music and Top Mule Music administered by The Loving Company. International copyright secured. All rights reserved. Reprinted by permission of Hal Leonard Corporation. © 2003 Super Id Music (ASCAP)/Sassy Mule Music (ASCAP)/Top Mule Music (ASCAP) (all administered by The Loving Company), et al. All rights reserved. Used by permission. Don Pfrimmer, Richie MacDonald, Ron Harbin. © 2004 Don Pfrimmer Music (ASCAP) administered by Wixen Music Publishing, Inc. All rights reserved. Used by permission. Mr. Richie MacDonald administered by ole Media Management L.P. o/b/o ole Red Cape Songs (ASCAP).

A FREE eBook edition is available with the purchase of this print book

CLEARLY PRINT YOUR NAME IN THE BOX ABOVE

Instructions to claim your free eBook edition:
1. Download the BitLit app for Android or iOS
2. Write your name in UPPER CASE in the box
3. Use the BitLit app to submit a photo
4. Download your eBook to any device

ISBN 978-1-63047-130-9 paperback
ISBN 978-1-63047-131-6 eBook
ISBN 978-1-63047-132-3 hardcover
Library of Congress Control Number:
2014933860

Cover Design by:
Chris Treccani
www.3dogdesign.net

Interior Design by:
Bonnie Bushman
bonnie@caboodlegraphics.com

In an effort to support local communities, raise awareness and funds, Morgan James Publishing donates a percentage of all book sales for the life of each book to Habitat for Humanity Peninsula and Greater Williamsburg.

Get involved today, visit
www.MorganJamesBuilds.com.

Habitat for Humanity®
Peninsula and
Greater Williamsburg
Building Partner

DEDICATION

This book is dedicated to my mother. If I could build a monument to any person on this earth, it would be to her. She is the epitome of womanly strength, character and compassion. Her heart and mind are irrefutable evidence that angels exist. She was and still is my hero and the heartbeat of our family. I struggle here, knowing that my frail words cannot do her justice.

Mom,

My strength, character and values have been inspired mostly from you. For what it is worth, let this book stand as my humble tribute to all you selflessly gave to me and everyone in our family for so many years.

TABLE OF CONTENTS

PREFACE

Jim laced his boots. They were just the way he liked them—old. Creased with mortar dust, they were soft, but thick and rugged with new laces. He straightened. His icy blue eyes and peppered hair contrasted against his sun and wind-burnt skin. He lifted his canvas bag of tools as his mind repeated his proud mantra from Henry the 8th: "Once more into the breach dear friends."

Then, his long stride carried him over the threshold into the cutting Pennsylvania winter. The wooden screen door smacked shut behind him, sealing in the scent of coffee mingled with the sweet steam of the old farmhouse's only working bathroom.

Jim lived for mornings like this. The brisk air snatched away any sleepiness the coffee had not already remedied. His step quickened toward the gravel lane where his old Ford LTD waited for him, heat running.

Although he was tender at heart and a life-long student of scripture and history, Jim was a tough man. He had always surrounded himself with other tough men. It was one of the things that resonated with his spirit. He loved his job building with bricks. The physical demands, the nature of the jobsite, the culture of the workers. It was all part of him. He had tried his hand at other trades over the years——executive, pastor, car salesman——especially when money got tight and he had to consider his family. But he always found his way back to masonry, the job he loved. He prided himself on his grass roots. He was a man's man, strong, streetwise, and inventive. He was nobody's fool. His ingenuity and analytical mind gave him insight into people's real motivations. He had a knack for cutting through to the heart of a matter. Each word he spoke counted. He did not waste language. He understood its power.

As he neared his running car, his second oldest son rounded the corner of the barn and headed in the direction of the driveway, steamy breath puffing alongside him in the cold morning air. Lanky and tall, Cory had an overgrown frock of dark brown hair and vibrant blue eyes. He was a very driven teenager, always immersed in some project, adventure, or way to make money. This morning, he leaned a bit under the weight of his backpack. He was on his way to meet his friends at the high school gym to lift weights in hopes of added even an ounce of muscle to his awkward, slender frame.

When Cory saw his Dad, he smiled and walked over to say goodbye for the day. As he approached, Cory looked down and his smile turned to a grim expression.

"Dad, we need to do something about those boots."

"Why? They are exactly the way I like them."

"I know, Dad, but I have a pair of hiking boots in the same kind of condition. I love them, but they have one big problem. They have no reinforcement in the toe and when I kick a rock or a root as I'm hiking, it kills my toes. I can see the leather thinning on the front of yours and working around bricks and scaffolding all day, it looks like you keep knocking your toes around too."

Jim looked down at his boots and wiggled his toes around inside the old leather.

"What we both need is comfortable boots with reinforced toes. Kick-proof boots. Besides, you keep replacing the laces because your grommets are bent and are cutting through a pair of laces every two weeks. That shouldn't be happening. Down at the Army/Navy store, they have used boots that are just barely broken in. Still in great shape, almost new, but with a strong toe, great ankle support and smooth grommets to save your laces. The grommets are also larger, so they can handle stronger laces, the kind you need. You should go down there this weekend."

Jim was now looking down at his boots and frowning. He hadn't considered that he could get another pair of boots that were already broken in, but might save his toes and laces. Cory also knew what he was talking about. An avid hiker, Cory hit the trails every weekend, whenever he could. For his age, he certainly knew the value of decent boots. The Army/Navy store in their hometown was synonymous with good quality and, as an ex-Marine, Jim loved the rugged items on the shelves.

As he considered his trusty footwear, something occurred to him. His frown broke into a broad smile and he looked up at his son. "Cory, you are a talented kid, good at a lot of things. You will probably have many jobs in your life, but if you don't make your living as a salesman, you will have missed your calling. I'll go to the store this weekend." And with that, Jim got into his car and drove away.

As Cory watched the car depart, gravel crunching under its tires, he reviewed his Dad's words. A salesman? As far as Cory was concerned, he was going to be an expert carpenter, electrical engineer, hiker, traveler, adventurer and DJ. "Salesman" sounded about as interesting as "dentist". He turned and walked out across the adjacent field, headed toward school.

What Cory failed to realize at age 14, was that he had just perfectly executed the age-old formula for selling a product. His father was right. Cory intuitively understood and sales would be his greatest calling, one filled with adventure and challenge—a calling that would pull on every skill he possessed.

INTRODUCTION

There is a formula that works. Whether you want to hit the big time and sell on television or want to create an online presentation video to spike your sales and minimize your returns, you can do it with the right perspective and a solid plan. Within these pages lie both. I will share with you what I have culled from selling well over 200 products on retail television and infomercials.

Yes, there are hazards to success. But they can be circumvented if you know they exist. After 15 years in the industry as a director, videographer and on-air presenter, I have a unique perspective. I know both the front and back sides of the lens. I know what works as both the talent and as the technical crew. I have enjoyed great success in both arenas. Having sold more than $100,000,000 worth of products in the past five years alone, I am going to sit down with you and show you what works.

WHAT TO DO

Chapter 1

THE MOMENT
OF TRUTH

It's your turn. In a moment, you'll be in front of the camera with your dream product—the one you know could sell like wildfire if only you get the chance to show it. The show host welcomes you onto the set and you step into the spotlight. There she is, along with all those lenses, looking for a response. You know everything there is to know. You reviewed every detail. Why is your face flushed—your throat so tight? The lights are blinding. What did she say again? You tell yourself, *Stick to the plan*. Wait—was there a plan? In that moment, the infinite directions you could take hit you like an overwhelming landslide. You can hear the ticking of the clock in your mind. You open your mouth to speak . . .

The time zoomed by. How could it go so fast? It felt like you barely said anything. There was so much more to say, but you did not get the chance. You had cool things to show, but you never touched them. You started and it was over. The music swelled and you were asked to step out. The lights are on another now. It is his turn. You stand on cold sidelines where the lights don't reach, the dim glow of the monitors your only company. It did not happen the way you imagined. You instinctively know the numbers will not add up in your favor. How can anyone have success under such conditions?

I equate what I do to speed chess. There is a clock ticking. I know the movement of each one of my pieces and the board so intimately, that no matter what the other player does, I can adapt quickly and stay on target for success. If she says this, I go there. If she says that, I change tactics. The goal is the big win. Some people get there almost every time. Others move their pieces, scorn the weight of the clock's tick and feel robbed of success. They blame the elements beyond their control—the person they were working with or the team around them. In reality, it was their own fault, but they are not to blame. There is precious little training to be had in this field and most people who are good at video and television sales hide their secrets behind smiles. The TV presenter's world has tons of comradery, but it can also seem very unfair. One person's product could be another's tomorrow. Months of preparation can go right down the drain if the pitch is just slightly off the mark. I have watched it happen over and over. If you are a professional presenter, you need to bring you're A-game every single time and you need to know how to continually achieve big wins! Here is where you need to start.

Chapter 2

BEGIN WITH THE END IN MIND

Every day I step on the air, I know exactly who I am talking to. I am having a three-way conversation with my host and the person on the other end of the camera lens. That person is a stay-at-home woman with disposable income. She aspires to be trendy, healthy and beautiful. She prides herself on having product solutions and getting values she can share with her friends. She is savvy. She is a shopper who knows prices and how to spot a deal. She loves her home and wants her guests to feel embraced by it when they walk through the door or up her walkway. Most of all, she loves to step out her door and find that little brown package sitting on her porch once or twice a week. She anticipates its arrival from the moment she commits to buy.

When I begin a presentation, the foremost thing in my head is who I am talking to. When you speak to a person, your body language, your tone and inflection, your eyes, and how you dress all convey a powerful message. I want to make that woman on the other end of the camera feel special, like I have taken time out of my day just for her and respect that she has done the same for me. I want her to know I am happy to see her and glad she has stepped into our little circle for the conversation to follow.

It takes a bit of imagination to look at a camera lens and see all that. I have been doing it long enough that it is effortless at this point. I rarely see the lens any more. I see my viewer. If I did not know who I was speaking to, I would never be as successful.

You cannot include all of humanity in your demographic. With the internet, you may very well reach all of them, but you cannot cater to a Dallas construction worker and a Manhattan debutant. You need to spend some time imagining who would find your product most desirable, and then *speak to that person personally*. Begin planning your presentation knowing who the end viewer will be. It will be the framework that could determine which demonstrations to do and which ones to omit, which points are most valuable and which ones are superfluous.

You need to spend some time imagining who would find your product most desirable, and then *speak to that person personally*.

I once heard a smart businessman say "Write the brochure for the company you want to have, then go create it." People usually do things the other way around. We create something first, then try to create the brochure to describe our creation. With presentation video, you do not create the video, and then hope to reach the right customer. Instead, you create the profile for the customer you want to reach, and then go reach him/her with your video! Is she a mother? Is he a bachelor? Does he travel? Has she rarely left her hometown? Understand as many of these nuances as is necessary to close your eyes and see your customer's face. It makes for a far more believable presentation. It should not take you long. You know your product. Spend 15 minutes jotting down the profile of your buyer, then tell everyone involved in the scripting process. Hand that profile off to your talent, director and videographer. It will help craft the feel of your presentation. It is easier to trust someone when they have taken the time to understand how you think and why. Your customer will subconsciously appreciate the effort and you will be far more likely to resonate with their instincts for trust and belief.

Activity

Customer Profile:

Is your customer primarily (60%-70%) male or female?

_____

How old is he/she? _____

Does he/she have children? _____

If so, what ages? _____
Give some examples of other products he/she owns
and likes:

_____

_____

_____

_____

Does he/she work? _____

What is his/her income? _____

Does he/she live in a specific climate? _____

If so, where? _____

What does he/she drive? _____

What are his/her hobbies? _____

Does he/she shop online, at the mart stores or locally own
shops? _____

On holidays, does he/she go to visit his/her family or do they come to him/her? _____

How does he/she dress? _____
These questions are just to get you thinking. Invent some of your own!

Chapter 3

BENEFITS NOT FEATURES

> *"At the end of the day, people won't remember what you said or did, they will remember how you made them feel."*
>
> —Maya Angelou

The front door swung open and we were immediately caught in the embrace of this beautiful home. The scent of cinnamon was in the air, a soft classical guitar played on the house-wide PA system and large glass doors across the room opened to a view that was breathtaking. When we pulled into the driveway, I had wanted to march straight around the house and survey its exterior, but I was delayed by the realtor who insisted I start with the inside and led me to the front door. He was smart. He wanted my first moment on this property to grab me and he succeeded. The view from the front door toward the rear of the living room was a perfectly framed masterpiece. The travertine entryway stepped down onto gleaming cherry wood floors, which stretched 20 feet across the room to the wall of glass through which I was looking. The pool and elevated hot-tub sat just above the backyard which dropped away into a pristine lake. No other homes were visible from this angle. I was captivated. Elizabeth caught her breath and squeezed my arm without releasing her grip. I knew she was feeling the same thing. The realtor stepped out of the entry way and conducted us through the home. We saw the extensive kitchen with its island sink and the garden tub surrounded by a curved wall of marbled glass block, sunlight spilling in. He offered us a water bottle and invited us to sit in the patio chairs and enjoy our refreshment. We listened to the geese on the lake and the soft trickle of the water spilling out of the hot tub and into the pool. We thought of the fact that we like to entertain, and this house would certainly accommodate that. The extra bedroom appealed to us. It simply wasn't fair to insist that our teenagers share a bedroom. Besides, their homework time was far more efficient when they were separated from each other while doing it. We thought of how restrictive the back yard was at our current home and how this one was certainly a better place for our kids to grow up. Hadn't we seen other children playing as we drove into the neighborhood? We were certain that lots of families lived nearby and our kids would have tons of playmates.

All these justifications ran through our heads like lightning. We talked excitedly about them, and our enthusiasm spread between us as we fed off each other. We would later use all those same reasons to inform our family and friends why we bought that house—why we got ourselves into a mortgage that stretched us beyond our financial plan for a new home. You see, we bought that home long before any of our justifications took root. We bought that home somewhere between the front door and the back porch.

I get to see many products—not merely the ones I represent, but tons of others that move through TV network halls. Those products are pitched to network buyers and considered by marketing companies for television retail or infomercial. I interact with lots of other presenters. We exchange thoughts and ideas on what worked on-air and what didn't. We are there to represent the best points of a product and help the viewer to understand why it can make a difference in their lives. You may notice I did not say, "We are there to help the viewer understand all the cool things a product can do." Although those cool things are a big part of any presentation, it is the perspective given as to why those cool things are important that makes the difference. Let me explain.

In 2012, IBM posted an article for their mid-sized business program. It stated "Buyers do not make logical, rational buying decisions. They make emotional decisions and then justify those decisions by rationalizing them after-the-fact. This is true even if they use a spreadsheet to evaluate suppliers and solutions. This is why you must develop the trusted relationships that put you in front of the buying process and in front of a deal."

What IBM recognized is a principle as old as time itself and one that surrounds you every day. The heart dominates the buying decision. Look at every billboard, every television commercial, every car lot, product package and magazine ad through those heart-shaped glasses. You will see exactly what I am talking about. Consumer's emotions are constantly bombarded. Every company selling something is trying to yank people's heart strings one way or another. Those companies are looking for an emotional response to build their case upon: anger at injustice or poor quality, sympathy for loved ones, trepidation at the unknown or possible suffering, the promise of relaxation, stress relief or avoidance of work. There are hundreds of scenarios, but all them are built on one purpose: generate an emotional reaction in the consumer and the rest is a walk in the park.

The heart dominates the buying decision.

Once there has been an emotional shift in your customer, their own logic will do the heavy lifting from that point on. They will listen intently to all the reasons they should buy from you and their own mind will strive to justify what the heart already believes and wants. If they do not buy right then, they will think about it afterward and might even kick themselves later for not buying. It is the reason that home buyers put themselves in terrible mortgages just to get the house they fell in love with and imagined their family living in. It is the reason car buyers will make astronomical payments just to see the look on their friends faces when they pull up. Those buyers have already run through these scenarios in their own imaginations long before the paperwork was signed. The heart led the way. It was then up to the brain to find every justification possible to give the heart its desire. As a presentation scripter, you are not primarily appealing to the intellect. Foremost, you are appealing to the heart.

A list of features creates no such response. Your product might do amazing things, but if all you focus on is what it CAN do and not WHY that is important in the life of your viewer, you will have missed the boat. Benefits should be your focus, not features. You should always start a point with, "Here is the difference my product can make in your life," then follow up with "let me show you how." Benefit first. The feature is merely a reason why that benefit exists. When you take this approach, you are catering to the emotions of your viewer. You are pulling at their heart and helping them to emotionally engage with your offer. You are pulling them to the screen and making them silently say "Wow, I could use that!" or "Wow! My daughter could use that!"

Benefits should be your focus, not features.

A few weeks ago, I was coaching a new presenter on how to sell her line of perfumes. Perfume is a tough one. People do not have smell-a-vision. There is no demonstration that is going to visually convey how awesome a perfume is. A presenter has the bottle, maybe a few props showing off the scents, possibly some support video showing how the perfume is made, but that's about it. Ninety percent of the presentation is all about expressions and verbiage. This new guest was stuck on talking about the perfume's middle and top notes (the recognizable scents like rose, citrus, etc.). She primarily wanted to go through the manufacturing process and the company's philosophy when creating a new perfume. I coached her otherwise. Although the information she had was important and could be peppered throughout her presentation for flavor, what would really sell her perfume was an appeal to how a woman would feel wearing her scent. Would that woman walk into a room feeling confident? Would she feel desirable or sexy? Would she feel youthful or fun? This is how you sell perfume. You convey the emotions when using it. You help the viewer to daydream about wearing it by suggesting scenarios and their outcomes with the perfume on.

"Can you imagine going out for the evening with your significant other and he is riveted to you? He cannot tear himself away from you and his hands seem to wander more than usual! Can you imagine how desirable you would feel? Our scent gives you that. No matter what you are wearing, it drops you right into your sexiest evening gown and heels with a press on the sprayer."

You see, that saleswoman wanted to hinge her whole presentation on features, but the benefits, or the results of those features, were the real selling point.

Unfortunately, inventors and manufacturers sometimes lose sight of this fact. When they originally had the idea for their product, it was based on a benefit that was missing in the marketplace. They wanted to improve someone's life by reducing their workload, giving them more time, solving a problem or saving them money. But, once the design process began, their focus became how to make this benefit a reality. That's where the product's features came in. Certain features result in a predictable benefit. Although the benefit was the initial idea that emotionally resonated with the inventor, the features become consuming and the totality of the manufacturing process. By the time the inventor could hold the product in his hands, he was personally so invested and proud of the multitude of features it had, he lost sight of the original idea. Features became the focus of all his sales. I have even had manufacturers brag to me for lengths of time on the design of their packaging and ask me to point it out within the first few minutes of sales time! Granted, great packaging helps establish a brand and create a unique customer experience (Steve Jobs knew the truth of this), but that should never be your focus. Get back to the reason the product was created in the first place—the benefits. Create that emotional response in your customer. Help them test drive your product in their imagination. Help them realize how it will improve their life. Help their emotions to engage. Then, give them the "How." That is the epicenter of all sales and should be the primary focus of a great product presentation.

Help them test drive your
product in their imagination.

Activity

What is your customer's problem that your product solves?

_____

What is the solution that your product provides?

_____

How is your customer going to feel experiencing that solution? (Be detailed)

_____

How can you describe your solution to help your customer emotionally engage?

_____

Invent a short scenario describing that solution at work in your customer's life and the feelings associated with it.

_____

_____

_____

_____

Name the 5 most important features of your product:

1. _____

2. _____

3. _____

4. _____

5. _____

Name 5 benefits associated with those features:

1. _____

2. _____

3. _____

4. _____

5. _____

Chapter 4

KEY POINTS

As you may have guessed by now, I have known two fathers in my life. Andy left our family when I was two years old. The earliest memories I have are blurry snapshots of being with him as he blew glass in his craft store. After the divorce, I saw him for a few weeks each year when my brother and I would visit. When I turned 18, he took me in and gave me a springboard to start my college career and adult life. I was handed the chance to know him intimately, and I was so impressed. Gentle and loving with a million stories, he is a wonderful man and I owe him much.

My second father was Jim. He raised me from ages 6 to 18. You met him in this book's introduction. He bandaged my skinned knees, taught me my values and how to work hard, inspired my passion for the outdoors, helped me with my homework and read classic books to me before bed at night. He was the Dad that raised me and had much to do with who I am. He passed away in 2004. I miss him dearly.

I lay this out so you know the cast of characters. I will refer to my family throughout the book and I thought you should know who they are.

Within this cast, Jim was the intellectual, philosopher, student, bricklayer and pastor. He delighted in the teachings of others who he felt could unwrap the mysteries of the scripture and make them simple to understand. His favorite teacher was a pastor and missionary named Malcolm Smith who came to the streets of New York City during the Christian Charismatic Movement of the 1960s and 70s. I can still remember hearing the distinctive British accent of Malcolm's voice coming from the little cassette-player speaker behind my parents' bedroom door and knew, it was not okay to even knock. This was time set aside for nourishing the soul and they were not to be interrupted. Malcolm could teach for an hour on one verse. My Dad had been to one of Malcolm's weekend retreats where the topic was the New Testament book, Philemon. Just in case you are not a student of the Bible, Philemon fits on a single page and is only 25 short verses long. My Dad used to laughingly say that Malcolm Smith was the only man who could spend 3 full days on Philemon and make them riveting! Malcolm had a way of explaining things that always stayed on target with the lesson topic, but found different ways to support it from many, many angles. Give him a verse and he could teach on it for five seconds, five minutes or five hours. It really depended how long you were willing to listen. Malcolm always had a few key points within his message and would come back to them over and over again after giving you some new nugget of insight to consider. Each of his messages was a simple one. He would often encapsulated them in a few reiterated words used every so often within his teachings to remind his listeners about the context of the lesson and what they needed to consider. He knew his key points.

I sometimes compare what I do as a presenter to creating a billboard. Professional advertising agencies who create billboard ads know that whatever text they decide to put up on that billboard, they have six precious seconds to deliver the message. That's about six words. Anything more that that is a waste of space and effort. It will fly by and the driver will have no idea what it said. Think of the agents sitting around a table suggesting ideas. Think how intimately they must know the product they are presenting. It takes a great representative to know everything about a product. It takes an expert to be able to deliver the essence of it in just a few words. More than a slogan, but less than a sentence. Not easy. It is difficult to cull all the great features of a product down to the ones that really resonate with a customer, but it must be done.

One of the first products I ever presented on television was a vacuum that was a big name in the UK, but no one in the US had ever heard of it. It was also expensive. At a price of over $300, it was a tough sell. Well-known US brands were so much less. I had crammed my head with every detail of my vacuum. As far as I was concerned, I could have done an hour on the item. I had so much I wanted to say. I was convinced I had a good plan and was given 18 minutes to make my case. Ready, set, go! I was projected to sell 200. I sold 40. After a short discussion with my producer, I discovered that more people started ordering each time I showed the retractable cord and the size of the dirt bin. So, for my next presentation, I decided to make those two points my focus. I must have pulled the cord out, hit the button and let it snap back into the vacuum 50 times over. I also pulled the dirt bin out and came up with a demonstration to show how many pounds of sand it could hold. The next airing quadrupled in sales from our first attempt! Although the exorbitant price of that vacuum and its obscurity never made it a big contender on television, I learned a powerful lesson. Pick two or three big points and hit them over and over again. Viewers get lost if there are too many details and features. They cannot digest them all. Keep things simple and impactful. Your viewers are not buying a product to solve 20 problems. They are buying it to solve one or two. Focus on the main reasons your product stands above the rest and show that it does its primary function well. You can pepper-in other features throughout the presentation for seasoning, but you should always circle back to your big points in short order. Reinforce the big bullets. Keep it simple. If it is easy to understand, you will sell more!

Pick two or three big points and
hit them over and over again.

Although it is rare, sometimes one big point is enough to sell a product. I have watched many cleaning products sell enormous volume by making the same point over and over. They convince the buyer by stating, "This product cleans better than the one you are currently using." However, the multitude of demonstrations used by the presenter are each very different. He/She will clean grease, then permanent marker, then spray paint, then nail polish, then carpet, then tile, then a stove top, then a car seat. The message is the same key point, but the product features appear to change each time a different substance or surface is cleaned.

Decide what your key points are. If you could only say three things to your potential buyer and then you had to stay quiet while they considered your product, what three things would you mention? What makes your product distinctive in the marketplace? What does your product have that no one else's does? What does it do exceptionally well and why? Dig deep for these points. Write them down. They are the heartbeat of your presentation plan.

Activity

In the last chapter, you laid out the five most important benefits of your product. Keeping those in mind, hone in on three key points. These are the heartbeat of your presentation.

Key Point #1

_____

Key Point #2

_____

Key Point #3

_____

_____

Chapter 5

HAVE A
CATCH PHRASE

In 1922, a Minnesota man accidently spilled a wheat bran mixture onto a hot stove. By 1924, we knew that accident as the breakfast cereal Wheaties. On Christmas Eve of 1926, General Mills was about to pull Wheaties off the store shelves. They had tried to sell it, but it simply wasn't popular or profitable. Within a year, all that changed and now Wheaties is a breakfast staple across the globe. What made the difference? A jingle. General Mills had concocted the short sing-songy phrase, "Have you tried Wheaties? They're whole wheat with all of the bran. Have you tried Wheaties? For wheat is the best food of man." No one had ever heard a jingle before. It summed up the appeal as to why a person would want to "try Wheaties," in a few short phrases. Just as General Mills was about to dig a grave for Wheaties, they saw a spike in the popularity of the cereal in the regions where this short marketing song was being broadcast, so they decided to run the catchy phrase on radio nationwide. Sales went through the roof. Granted, the jingle has some elements to it that make it stick in your head. Music and rhyme are not components used in product presentations. However, the catch phrase itself, when repeated several times throughout a presentation, will help your customer remember the primary reasons they want your product! Not only does it help you refocus the presentation on what's important each time it is stated, the catch phrase stays with your viewer in the back of their head for recall later. When they share your product with a friend, it will be the first thing they mention. When they are comparison shopping, they will hold other brands up against the benefits of your catch phrase. It is a powerful tool!

The catch phrase stays with your viewer in the back of their head for recall later.

I sell a product that it is a jump start system for your car. At the beginning of each presentation, I engage my viewer by relating to their experiences when their battery dies. Then I say "This is a spare battery for your car that will have you back on the road in ten minutes without ever leaving the safety, comfort and convenience of your driver's seat." That's when the calls start rolling in. I proceed to show them how the jumpstarter works and why, but that catch phrase is repeated two to three times throughout the presentation to reinforce the uniqueness of the product and give some context to the other features.

I also sell a battery regenerator for alkaline batteries (non-rechargeable). At the top of each presentation, right after I relate to my viewers the emotional problem with buying batteries, I say "This device will regenerate your alkaline batteries back to 99.5% of their original power and will do it dozens and dozens and dozens of times over for each individual battery." The phone lines usually explode right about that time. I say that phrase two to three times throughout the presentation. I keep circling back to it. In less than ten seconds, I have given my viewer the primary emotional and logical reasons they must have that product.

For three years at networks in both the US and Canada, I sold the world's number one gaming console. When the presentation began, I would always play the game in the background while the TV host set up the offer. Then she would introduce me and I would turn around and say "This is a full multi-media console that brings family game night back to your home using space age technology! It tracks the movement of your body so you never have to learn how to use a remote to play. Just jump in front of the screen with your kids and start moving!" I would circle back to this statement two to three times during the presentation, sometimes changing the wording slightly so it did not sound tiringly verbatim. The first time I presented that gaming console, it was the North American launch of the product. I sold 1,600 systems in 17 minutes. That presentation broke all kinds of sales records for a gaming product. Although the network's merchandising team was excited about the new product, they never anticipated the monstrous success of that first airing. The network had to start the following hour of cookware products three minutes early! There were no more game consoles left to sell! Over the following two years, that game system was in the top three most money-making electronic items offered at the network during the Christmas season. The manufacturer of that console had created a revolutionary new technology and I had to frame it correctly for the viewer. It was not just a gaming system for kids. It was full multi-media console that brought the family together for a night of fun!

Before that game console hit the market, I had the same success with another system. Much of this had to do with the how the viewer interpreted the product once I had set the stage with my repetition of the catch phrase. "This is the game system that gets you up and gets you moving. Wherever you move the remote is where the action happens! Whether you are a teenager or a grandparent, you will never have so much fun playing video games with the family!"

I could give you hundreds of examples of presentations with such phrases. Every product must have a catch-phrase, a short one to three sentence phrase that encompasses the essence of why that product is unique. It should resonate with the viewer's emotions, and make them relate to the presenter and understand the significance of the product. Often, this phrase is the one of the first things out of the presenter's mouth, the last thing they say and is peppered throughout the presentation. It is a critical component of any successful presentation plan. Omit this one detail and you will find yourself standing in line with all the other wishy-washy presentations that do marginal sales and wish they could be a super-star!

Activity

Now that you have analyzed your product's primary benefits, create 1–2 short sentences that encapsulate that reasons someone would want your product.

List your 3 primary benefits identified in the activity from chapter 4:

1. _____

2. _____

3. _____

Now merge these 3 benefits into a statement that helps people to instantly understand why they want your product. Remember, this is an emotional appeal. You are identifying with your customer and providing a solution that matters to them!

This is the_____(product type) that

_____

_____

_____

_____

Chapter 6

HAVE A GOOD PRESENTER

In May of this past year my family and I were on our boat, a modest 22 foot cabin cruiser. We were navigating the labyrinth of canals in Florida's intra-coastal waterway, heading for John's Pass marina, where we planned to grab dinner at a dockside restaurant and watch the sunset. It had been an awesome day filled with snorkeling, Caribbean music, crystal waters and family. As we neared John's Pass, I feared I might have missed the turn leading to the restaurant, so I pulled out of the channel and began consulting my GPS. A few minutes later, a Sherriff's boat pulled up next to me and the lone officer on board announced that he was going to give us a pop-inspection of our safety gear. He asked for my registration and a life-preserver for each person on board. No problem. Check. He asked to see my air horn and VHF radio. Check. No issues so far. He asked for my fire extinguisher. I produced it immediately. He checked the date and announced that it was expired. I had no idea. He then asked for my flare gun. Because I had young children on board, I had opted not to carry a flare gun. Besides, I thought it was optional as long as I had an air horn and VHF radio. He informed me that it is mandatory. I few minutes later, I was watching his boat depart, holding a $93 ticket in my hand. Although the experience was not a positive one, I did not let it cloud my mood. After all, it was less than $100 and I was prepared with everything else he had asked for. The family and I proceeded to dinner.

When we got back to the dock later that evening and pulled the boat up onto the trailer, I looked for the ticket, but could not find it. I decided that I would wait for daylight and do a more thorough inspection. The next day, the kids and I tore the boat apart. We looked under every seat cushion, inside every cup holder, everywhere. We then looked in the truck with the same thoroughness. Nothing. We checked in all the bags of towels, snacks and lotion that had been on board with us. Still nothing. I resigned myself to the fact that the ticket must have blown overboard on the way back from John's Pass and was currently floating somewhere in the intra-coastal waterway. But, I knew this only meant that I would get a notice in the mail and have to pay a late fee. No biggie. I'd just wait for that letter—the one that never came.

Three months later, I had completely forgotten about the ticket all together. I was busy raising four kids and running a business. After telling myself that I would wait for the letter with the late fee, I flushed it from my mind, replacing it with the more urgent demands of the moment.

A letter arrived from an attorney's office informing me that they would be happy to represent me at my upcoming arraignment. Arraignment? What were they talking about? The day after, I received a court summons and my heart stopped.

"Mr. Bergeron. You are hereby ordered to appear before the Pinellas County Judicial court to answer for a 2nd degree misdemeanor charge of non-compliance."

"You can't be serious!"

Oh, they were serious all right. I told myself that this must be a mistake and called the courthouse to confirm. It was not. I was scheduled to appear in criminal court for my failure to pay a $93 boating ticket and was facing a 2nd degree misdemeanor on my record.

I priced attorneys, but they were all so expensive, to the tune of $700 to $800. I am a well-spoken, upstanding family guy who pays his taxes and has no record. Surely, when the judge heard the details of my infraction, all would be dismissed. I called the courthouse and quickly found out who I had to pay to satisfy my overdue ticket. I paid and filed the receipt in the paperwork I planned on presenting to the judge. I figured that it showed good faith in paying before my hearing. I then sat back in confidence, waiting for the day of the arraignment to arrive.

I stood as the honorable Judge W. entered the courtroom and felt this entire situation was almost laughable. The judge would roll his eyes when he found out how the system had railroaded me and the entire thing would be dismissed and expunged. Mine was the first name on the list. I was called and stepped through the small wooden door and up to the podium before the court. That is when everything went sideways.

"Mr. Bergeron, I must inform you that this is an arraignment, not a trial. I am not here to listen to any details regarding your case, I am simply here to get your plea and sentence you or schedule you for a trial. You are charged with a 2nd degree misdemeanor of non-compliance. How do you plea?"

I stood there having no idea how to proceed. Did I fail to pay the ticket? Yes. That makes me guilty. I certainly cannot say not-guilty. That would be false. I could not claim no-contest. That means I am not admitting guilt or lack of guilt. I knew I had not paid. My integrity won out. "Guilty, your honor."

"Ok, Mr. Bergeron. Let it be entered into the record that Mr. Bergeron has pleaded guilty to the charges against him. What sentence does the State recommend?"

The state prosecutor stood up behind me and said "We recommend a fine of $500 to be paid immediately and the charge against him to be filed as part of Mr. Bergeron's permanent record."

The judge asked if I understood this sentence. My heart was in my shoes. I was ready to weep openly. I said "Yes, your honor." He then asked me if I was aware of the PTI program. I said I was not. He explained that because I had no previous record, I would qualify for a state program that would require six months of probation and community service and would cost $300, but would result in all charges being dropped against me. I elected to proceed with PTI and walked out of the court room utterly depressed and defeated.

Since that day, I have acquired an attorney to plead my case. It has ended up costing me far more than if I had simply engaged him from the start. My attorney must now back-track and try to undo the damage I did by trying to represent myself. How could I have avoided this nightmare? How could I have walked away feeling in control of the situation rather than spiraling? I should have had a good attorney from day one. I should have had a good presenter.

I have worked with more than 200 products and their vendors in just the past five years. I have sold tools, various electronics, lawn and garden items, outdoor decor' items, children's toys, appliances, floor-care items, cleaning supplies, auto accessories, holiday decorations, lighting, video games, telephones and lots of miscellaneous items hard to categorize. Half the time, I am working with an experienced vendor who recognizes how crucial good talent is and the art behind presenting an item well. The other half the time, I am working with someone who is new to television or video retailing and thinks that his/her understanding of the product is unsurpassable and he/she is the obvious choice as talent. Very few times is that person correct.

When the latter case occurs, my phone rings because any national network has a branded image to uphold and not every face or voice is one for television. However, there was a time, earlier in the days of television retail, when many retail networks would allow almost anyone on air. As late as 2000, I watched a guy covered in tattoos, with a tank top, a mullet (a decade past the time when they were cool, if they ever were) and bald crown go on air to present a vacuum. I cannot think of a single television retail station today that would allow such a thing. Your talent should be clean cut, easy on the eyes, vulnerable with their emotions, warm, inviting, experienced and pleasing to listen to. They should know the art of not just looking at the lens, but reaching through it, right into the room of the viewer. Not a spokesperson, a neighbor. Above all, they should have good credibility and be believable. Not every clean cut person is credible and believable. A viewer is very sensitive to the person speaking to them. Your presenter should cater to that viewer's sensitivities.

A viewer is very sensitive to the person speaking to them.

A solid presenter should be able to stay focused and do so with concise, but smooth, conversational verbiage. The world of live television retail is entirely unscripted. For the most part, presenters walk on air with a set of mental bullet points and a presentation plan. They execute that plan and speak to the appropriate points as the demonstrations call for them. At the same time, they are using their peripheral vision to take in several reference monitors displaying what is being shown live on TV and what is about to be the next shot. They are also monitoring the camera tally lights, small red lights above each camera showing which camera is online at the moment. They have a stage manager and crew who are behind the cameras and will, at times, signal the talent, alerting them to issues. The talent is wearing a small earpiece into which the director and producer are talking, giving updates on sales, providing cues to cameras and demonstration feedback. The talent keeps things light and conversational while listening to the host, who is on air at the same time. When you stack all this on top of a presentation plan and demonstrations that are being done simultaneously, you can imagine how easy it would be to feel overwhelmed and appear frozen on air.

There are celebrity hosts on air even now that cannot manage all these distractions. They break with protocol and insist on going without an earpiece or crew on the set. With non-celebrity presenters, who cannot wield the influence of the upper crust and must follow all protocols, they must be unwavered by the multitude of distractions. You can certainly tune into live TV retail at any time and tell whether the guest is experienced or not. Hosts often take over for a guest and minimize their input during the presentation if they feel the guest is not experienced or equipped to do the job well. Some hosts will even take over the demonstrations and pacing as well. Air time is extremely valuable. Success is measured in thousands of dollars per minute. The clock is ticking and every second counts. Each comment is carefully measured before a presenter decides to commit time to it and if things get off-track, it is usually intentional and very brief. It is an art to stay focused within all of these distractions, yet give each comment the slice of attention it needs.

Success is measured in
thousands of dollars per minute.

Pre-recorded videos are not nearly as demanding on the talent as live television, but there are still significant demands. Your production crew has a day rate. You will need to be wrapped up before the buzzer sounds or it will cost you, big time. Lights will be blazing in the presenter's face. The crew wants to wrap scenes efficiently and move on to the next one. If you hit take number 11 and your presenter hasn't nailed it yet, people will start getting exasperated. If you are shooting outdoors, managing daylight can be a concern. The longer a scene takes, and the more the daylight changes, the greater the challenge will be to edit the scenes later on. Scenes end up looking very different and editing them side by side in a video looks bad. There are also the temperature factors if you are shooting in the summer or winter. The longer a scene takes, the more likely your talent will sweat through that nicely ironed button-up or turn bright red and then blue from the cold. Unless you have seasoned talent who can smoothly improvise your product points without error, your talent will be reading a teleprompter, using an ear-prompter or trying to remember his/her lines. Whoever you choose as talent, that person should be able to keep his/her focus on the presentation and keep things feeling warm and natural for the viewer despite the conditions. They should be able to nail down a scene in a few takes. Their verbiage should feel natural, smooth and kind with a touch of urgency, but not too much. Buyers do not like blatant pushiness. Usually, a presenter's enthusiasm will suffice as your touch of urgency. Gone are the days of the carnival barker salesman: "Step right up! Order right now! Everyone wins!" (Like the first two decades of infomercials). Most of all, your talent should be experienced enough to stay utterly focused on the vision of the video, knowing what everyone is there to accomplish and sensitive to the needs of the client and crew. Professionals make this look easy, but it is not as easy as it seems, as you can tell from the outlines I've given.

A presenter's enthusiasm will suffice
as your touch of urgency.

Pre-recorded video has a different feel than live television. Viewers are used to a more polished look. They expect the clean results they are used to from the big brands. Those brands are the ones who get the most exposure and have set the standard. If you are going to compete in your market, you will need to produce the same kind of cleanliness in your video, or it will seem *low-budget, amateur and small time*— three ways you do not want your viewer to interpret your company! Hire great talent or find someone with natural ability and develop them through practice. They are the face of your product and company. Do not cheat on this point. It will cost you in the long run. There is a graveyard full of products somewhere, products that had talent who knew every nut, bolt and feature, but had neither the expertise to resonate with the viewer nor the ability to do the product justice on video.

Remember, TV retail networks pair products with presenters every day. Those networks are a great resource of experience within different categories of products. They also know people who have solid sales histories and their advice is valuable! That's a big plus! A product presentation is a short-term relationship between the viewer and the presenter. It is based on instinctual trust. Close your eyes and imagine: Who would I most trust immediately if I saw that person using my product and I walked up to ask them about it? Who would be the ultimate person to lead me through my product's benefits and help me walk away feeling good about my decision to buy from them? Whose recommendation would I most value?

Go find that person! There are agents in every big city that can provide polished talent. Ask them to help you.

It will negate quite a bit of frustration and searching. You should still be personally involved in the scripting of the presentation. In that phase of producing your video, you can offer your wealth of experience. Then, find the perfect person to deliver your message!

Find the perfect person
to deliver your message!

Activity

Who would you most immediately trust to tell you about your product, if you changed places with your customer? Is that person male or female, rugged or polished, single or part of a family, young or middle-aged? Explore these aspects. List ten characteristics of your perfect presenter below. You want to know exactly who you are shooting for.

1. _____

2. _____

3. _____

4. _____

5. _____

6. _____

7. _____

8. _____

9. _____

10. _____

Now, connect with a talent agent or, if you are selling on TV, ask the network for some recommendations based on your vision above.

Chapter 7

THE DEMO

Currently, there is a craze over portable Bluetooth speakers. Several brands have made big names for themselves overnight by delivering ultra-high quality audio in sheik, small, rechargeable packages. People want to share their music in a better way, rather than relying on their tiny cell phone speaker. However, this craze has not caught on very well in the world of live television retail. Many companies have taken a shot at it, but few have had any success. Even the big brands have done poorly. There is one exception. A speaker that has been able to pull its own weight, yet it is not from a big recognizable brand. It sounds great, has a 15 hour battery, is waterproof, dust-proof, freeze-proof, life-proof, and it has a great demo.

When I go on air with this speaker, I place it on a large plastic tray, start the music jamming and pour a pitcher of water right over it. The music never misses a beat. However, it is the next demo that lights the lines. I turn the speaker cabinet on its back, so the speakers themselves are pointing toward the ceiling. I then fill the top of the speaker cabinet with water, and basically flood the drivers and put them underwater. I hit play on some bass-heavy music and the speakers shoot the water a foot into the air! I continue to refill the speaker drivers as the water shoots out and the host steps back from the table to keep the spray at a distance. That is the moment the phone lines explode. It is an awesome speaker. I have a very strong audio background and know as much. But, it is that one demo that pushed the buyers over the edge.

I sell a brand of doormats that have been reviewed online by over 350 consumers and have earned close to the maximum score any product can receive. It is a great product. However, it is the demo that inspires people to pick up their phones or drop those doormats into their online shopping cart. At the beginning of each presentation, I pick up a boot that has dirt all over the sole. I scrub the boot against the doormat 3–4 times and it comes up perfectly clean. Then, I pick up the doormat and empty five pounds of dirt out of it that was already in the mat before I cleaned the boot. (Cue the phone lines.) Later in the presentation, I pour five pounds of dirt into my doormat, clean a boot to show that it still works and then empty that dirt on top of a cocoa-fiber mat (very popular style these days). It looks ridiculous. The cocoa fiber mat is almost invisible under the mountain of dirt on top of it. I move the dirt around with my hands, trying to make it go somewhere. It just lies on top and spills over the edges. The dirt has nowhere to go. Regardless of what I am saying at that moment, the demonstration tells a powerful story. I believe strongly in those doormats. They made a huge difference in my own home. But, without that demo, very few people would have had the chance to believe in them as strongly as I do.

I also sell a line of compression storage bags. You fill them up with towels, blankets, clothes, pillows, or other fabric items and then vacuum the air out of the bag, compressing your items down to 25% of their original size. They are air tight, water tight, bug-proof and the most durable bags on the market. They come with the best warranty in the industry (five years) and beat everyone else's price by a big margin. Seems like a no-brainer, right? Not until my viewers see the demo. I put one in a suitcase, fill the bag with a ton of random stuff like winter jackets, ski pants, sweaters, etc. The pile looks so huge that you tell yourself, *There is no way he will ever get that suitcase closed.* I then put the vacuum hose on the bag. Within 60 seconds, everything has shrunk into the suitcase and there is even room for shoes and a hairdryer. The demo is so compelling that callers begin running to their phones. Online shoppers begin throwing more than one set at a time in their shopping carts. It is all about the demo and the hosts I work with cannot wait for me to do it.

The demo is so compelling that
callers begin running to their phones.

I have a friend of mine who sells vacuums for a leading manufacturer. She does a demo that rivets me every single time. She sticks it to a wall. Did I mention it is an upright vacuum? She picks it up, swings it horizontally and puts it up against the wall next to her. Then, she lets go and it holds itself there on suction alone. The first time I saw her do that, I was blown away. She does it two or three times throughout her presentation. Each time she does it, the callers abandon all reservations and pick up their phone or run to their computer.

I have seen demos like this a thousand times. Small canister vacs that lift bowling balls, pressure washers that are shot into Plexiglas with special attachments, expanding hoses that spill out over the bucket they fit so nicely in a moment earlier, cleaners that remove dry spray paint, mops that absorb ridiculous amounts of liquid, hangers that can be bent in half and don't break. All of these presenters are trying to get one message across: "You have never experienced anything like this product before. It will revolutionize the way you live." It resonates with people emotionally. It makes them imagine that same kind of performance in their own home. In one fell swoop, that demonstration spoke the language of the perfect sell. It spoke to the emotions which make the buying decision, the intellect which searches for reasons to justify the purchase and the imagination which convinces both that they can't even conceive everything this product is capable of. Slam dunk!

Not every product is so demonstrable. Many products are all about the verbiage and delivery. However, if a demonstration can be conceived for your product to help people understand just how well it performs, a demonstration that shows off its most significant, unique feature, that demo can make all the difference. Producers, guests and hosts I work with all know that until the customer sees the product do its job, they will not buy. Until they see the vacuum clean the floor, the steamer remove the wrinkles or the cookware make a perfect stir-fry, they will not buy. First show that the product does its primary job (playing music or cleaning the boot). Then, knock their socks off with the demo they did not see coming. It is a key recipe for success! By considering each step I am outlining, you are stacking the deck in your favor. Great demos are a big part of your winning hand!

Activity

Let's script your top three demonstrations. The best demonstrations magnify your product's key points and benefits. You have already scripted both. Now list the primary ways your product can be shown in action accomplishing those key points so that your viewer can sense the emotional benefits of owning what you're selling!

1. _____

2. _____

3. _____

Explore ingenuitive ways to take the actions above and boost their visual impact. Then, go try your ideas. Cross out what doesn't work and circle what does! For example, if you sell an organic cleaner and your demonstration idea above was to clean the floor, your boosted idea below could be to clean axle grease off hardwood with a single spray!

1. _____

_____

_____

2. _____

_____

_____

_____

3. _____

_____

Chapter 8

THE TESTIMONIAL

John had no idea how to get out of this. The forest was deserted. In any other season, this dirt road snaking its way through infinite trees would have had a few adventurous people passing by. But the snow was deep, the weather freezing and only John's 4-wheel drive and big engine had gotten them this deep into the woods. Charlie sat in the passenger seat with his gloved hands tucked into his armpits for warmth, his hooded scalp resting against the rear window of the old pickup. John knew they were in trouble. He watched Charlie exhale slowly, his breath gusting in clouds toward the truck's visor. His eyes were closed as he tried to find a bit of Zen in place of panic. John knew his truck's battery had been acting sluggish lately. It had been turning the engine a bit more slowly each time he started it.

Walking out of these woods in such deep snow would be impossible. They had no provisions and it would take days of toiling to get to the closest paved crossroad. John knew that he and Charlie were not survivalists. They were seasonal hunters who counted on being back in their beds each night. They enjoyed a day's jaunt into the woods for some game and then back to the warmth of their homes and wives. He wouldn't even know where to start in keeping hypothermia from claiming Charlie and him before morning. The sun was already below the horizon and the temperature was dropping fast. In Michigan's Upper Peninsula, winter could be brutal. John kicked himself over and over. What 42 year old man takes his buddy this far into the woods in winter without a plan in case things go sideways? No generator, no sleeping bags, no heater—nothing. All he brought was a truck that won't run and a cell phone that is completely out of range. Stupid! He slammed his foot against the pedal in frustration. Charlie's eyes popped open, his head jerking forward.

"Damn it, John! You scared the piss outa me!"

"I'm such an idiot," John rasped.

"Yeah, you are at times," Charlie jabbed.

"Maybe a ranger will come by."

"I think not. Any ranger with half a brain is hunched over some hot coffee with a fireplace and a woman right now," Charlie said

"Margaret is going to kill me. She probably knows exactly what's happening right now. She's an intelligent girl and she's been telling me for weeks to get a new battery. If she only knew where we were, maybe she could send someone."

"You didn't tell her were we were headed? Doesn't that beat all! And here, I thought we had a glimmer of hope! God, John!"

"I know, you should use that shotgun on me! What about Sue?

"Really, John? She's a debutant. There is no hope for rescue there. Roper would be a better bet than Sue," Charlie said.

"Your dog? He's a Schnauzer!"

"Still a better bet," Charlie said as his head dropped back against the window.

John went quiet again. Margaret was not the super-outdoorsy type. She was more of the all-American soccer mom. Sunday potlucks at the park and backyard barbeques with the neighbors were more her speed. If she had any idea what kind of risk John was planning on taking, she would have called him an idiot too!

Suddenly, John's heart leapt into his throat! He just remembered something. He lurched across Charlie's lap and yanked open the glove compartment. He started emptying it onto the floor. Old maps, some random tools and a stick of deodorant avalanched between Charlie's knees.

"What the—" Charlie yelled as his head jerked forward once more.

"I just remembered. I think I have a—YES!"

John pulled out a small, red cylindrical canister and a cable.

"Margaret gave me this," John rejoiced.

"What is it?" Charlie asked doubtfully.

"It's a car jumpstarter!"

Charlie started laughing.

"Uh, John? There is now way in hell that little thing is getting this truck going again. I crap bigger than that."

"Yeah, well, it's worth a try. It's all we got," John replied.

John read the directions on the bottom of the jumpstarter.

"Turn on, plug in, wait ten minutes, turn key and go," John said.

He flipped the little switch forward on the cable adaptor, thrust it into the cigarette lighter socket in the truck's dash and then looked at his watch.

"Ten minutes," he reiterated.

"This is never going to work," Charlie said

"I told Margaret the same thing when she gave it to me. Picked it up from some shopping channel. One for each of our cars. I laughed at her. Told her there was no way. Maybe her little Euro car, but not my truck. Still, it's hope! That's the first we've had!"

Charlie was beginning to feel some anticipation as the hands on John's watch swung past minute six. He leaned toward the socket, looking at the little green LED glowing on the adaptor.

"Well, it's still going. I would have thought your truck would have sucked it dry by now."

Minute eight ticked past.

"C'mon, baby. Do your thing. My toes are numb and my nose is going to fall off." John's body trembled as the bitter cold swept through him. He looked out at the growing darkness. Degrees were dropping away every second. It would be below zero tonight.

Minute nine.

John and Charlie were now barely breathing. It was as if any movement or noise might take away from the chance of their salvation from this tiny cylinder. It did not make a sound. It just sat there, green light winking.

John watched as the second hand of his watch ticked painfully slow.

"Do you think we should give it 11 minutes just in case," John asked.

"I dunno. Maybe," Charlie said "We want to get everything it's got."

As the watch had neared 10 minutes, the little green light changed to yellow.

"Uh, I'd say that's a clear signal that we should turn the key," John said

"Do it," Charlie responded

"C'mon baby, please," John whispered as his hand closed on the key and he twisted.

John later called in to the shopping channel where Margaret purchased the jumpstarter -and gave his testimonial. He was convinced that he and Charlie had been done for. When the engine sprang to life, he and his friend yelled and grabbed each other in celebration. They were both convinced the "Mighty Jump" had saved them. Neither of them had any idea how they would have gotten out of there otherwise. Margaret, of course, capitalized on her wisdom and foresight by reminding John for years to come about how he had initially laughed at her.

I enjoy telling stories. Both the father that raised me and the father I barely knew until I moved in with him to start college were great storytellers. I have a bit of both of them in my blood. What you just read is based on a testimonial from a caller during a live TV presentation. I embellished the story to make it a more entertaining read, but both the emotions of the characters and the general scenario are accurate.

Imagine what the viewers thought after hearing that story. There I am on national television, holding that battery jumpstarter in my hand and claiming it will start any gas-powered consumer vehicle, regardless of its tiny size. Then, John calls in. By the end of that phone call, hundreds of people were on hold to get their own jumpstarter. We sold thousands in that airing, which lasted about 15 minutes. The power of the consumer's voice cannot be overstated. They want to hear from their peers. In retail television, every host, guest, producer, sales manager, buyer, planner and administrator knows that if you get a really great testimonial call, it can spike your sales like no other element in your presentation. Presenters will stop their demonstrations and pitches, hosts will derail their conversations and producers will add minutes to an item's timing if necessary just to take that call. If you are planning to sell on TV or create a great internet product sales video, a solid testimonial or two could be your greatest asset.

> The power of the consumer's
> voice cannot be overstated. They
> want to hear from their peers.

So, how do you get them? Simple. You give free samples of your product to people in exchange for their testimonial after they have had a chance to use it for a while. You can use friends, family outside of your home, or the first ten customers to approach your booth at a trade show. The point is to find people who are emotionally expressive and authentic. I advise against using anyone within your own household. The camera has a very critical eye. It will amplify a rehearsed response or staged scenario. It will make something planned look *extremely* planned. You don't want that. You want spontaneous, genuine experiences. Let people use your product without input or interference from you. Then, follow up with them and get their stories. If your product has an immediate result that can be experienced and commented on, have the camera and microphone standing by! If you are selling a knife that cuts through steel, don't wait to follow up later! The sooner you can grab someone's initial reaction on camera, the more impactful and genuine it will be! This does not work with every product. If you sell an air purifier, the user will have to use it over a period of time. But as a rule, you don't want to let too much time go by or you will dilute the testimonial. Get them as soon as it makes sense.

Give free samples of your product to people in exchange for their testimonial.

You can also give your product to professionals (tradesmen, doctors, attorneys) to get their feedback. You want to be careful, though. If you pay them anything for the testimonial arrangement, you will need to run a disclaimer at the bottom of your video stating that "this is a paid testimonial," in order to protect yourself legally. That disclaimer makes what is on the screen a bit less potent. Also, be sure that you file a signed talent release form (can be downloaded for free online) for each person you put on video. You don't want someone to insist that you remove their testimonial after it has been integrated into all of your media.

Unlike the rest of your video or presentation, the video testimonial can look a bit less polished. It still must maintain a decent amount of production value, but it can be done without much fanfare in your living room or on location as long as you keep a few things in mind:

- You want to use a good recording device that delivers crisp 1080 HD video with a real lens. Most compact video cameras are capable of this these days. Anything less and you will likely have a recording that will never make it to broadcast television (should you choose to use it in that environment someday). I would not advise using your mobile device unless you are creating internet video. The image from these devices will not be approved by network TV.

- Use a tripod or some other stabilizing device or surface. Nothing is more distracting or screams amateur than a video image bouncing around like a family video at a theme park. Keep your shot stable and locked in position.

- You want to be cognizant of lighting. You video should be well balanced without lighting that is too bright, too dark or with harsh shadows. Think of an overcast day or the inside of a well lit room with florescent lights. This is what you are shooting for. Of course, if your product is a beach umbrella and you are shooting on location, you might want that harsh sunlight to drive home the point of the umbrella! All these suggestions must be tempered with your own product knowledge.

- Be sure to white balance your recording device. If you are unsure what this is, refer to your device owner's manual or Google it. It is how your camera balances all of its colors so that people, for example, don't end up looking like Smurfs or Oompa Loompas! Daylight will give everything a bluish hue, while incandescent light in your house will make everything look orange. White balancing matches all your video colors to the kind of light you are shooting in. It is a function of almost every video camera. You will just need to find it in the camera menus. This is important to match the look of your testimonial to the rest of your video.

- Pick a simple backdrop. Do not let the area behind your subject look cluttered with kick knacks or distracting action. You want your viewer's focus to be solely on the person talking. Choose a background, if possible, that does not have distracting movement and allows the person talking to jump out at the viewer. The testimonial should be the most interesting thing on the screen. (This might not be entirely possible if you are grabbing people off Manhattan sidewalks to tell their story. But, if background action is not necessary within the context of your product, it should be avoided.)

- Have your testimonial subject look slightly off camera in an interview style. They should be talking to someone else, not the lens. The camera is just a spectator that is being ignored.

- Encourage your testimonial to express their full feelings when relating their experience. Remember, you will probably only be using a tiny snippet of everything they say. Let them talk. It is the best way to keep things spontaneous and organic. You will pick out your little gem of verbiage from amongst the whole monologue later on.

- Keep your testimonial framed tightly. Emotions resonate more strongly with viewers when they are experienced up close. Unless you are selling shoes, you should not be out any wider than a head to waist shot. Remember, the point is to share a person's emotions and experiences. Zoom the camera inside that person's personal space and your viewer will be far more riveted!

- You want your viewer to walk away feeling better about their world, not worse. When you select the piece of each testimonial that you want to use, keep things headed in a positive direction. In the world of live television, we take live testimonial calls. We screen those callers based on their account history and the nature of their story. We don't want to run the risk of some prankster getting their voice on national television just to see what they can get away with (it has happened before and ooooh man, could I tell you stories!). But, even with the screening process, callers often get on air and hurt sales more than help them. For instance, a lady will call in and say "I just love your air fresheners! Last month I was walking up the stairs and I fell, breaking both my kneecaps. Because my husband is convalescing, I was unable to clean up as usual, so the house began to smell. That's where your air fresheners came in. They were great for dealing with the odor!" Obviously, that is a severe example and not what you want. Your viewer walks away feeling awful. Your product is still great, but you have depressed their emotions about something else. You want them to walk away feeling hopeful and uplifted! Even if every other component of the testimonial is compelling, scrap it if you don't feel great about your world after listening to it. It is not worth the risk.

Once you have a few of those beautiful little nuggets of emotional authenticity in your pocket, you are in possession of one of the greatest tools you could ask for. Every bit of a product sales presentation is modeled around an emotional appeal. When you incorporate testimonials, you are appealing to your viewer's emotions through others who already own and use your product—and its affect is profound. Look at infomercials that have been running for the past 15 years on overnight television. The reason they are still there is because they got the formula right. They are hitting all the right emotional buttons. Pay attention to the multitude of interspersed customer testimonials. It works! Remember, you are attempting to encapsulate the best that your product has to offer. When someone is emotionally moved and enthusiastic about what their peers have said about an item they are considering, it could be the nudge that takes them to the "Buy Now" button!

Activity

Who would have the most profound emotional impact on your customer if they endorsed your product? Do a quick character analysis of who you imagine for your best testimonial. Who would be most compelling to hear from?

Male/Female, professional tradesman/average Joe, age bracket, etc.

_____

_____

_____

_____

_____

_____

_____

_____

_____

_____

_____

_____

Now list some names of people you know, people you could be connected to through others or people you need to find to get your testimonials.

Name	Contact Info	Testimonial Date/Time

Call these people. Ask them if they would be willing to help you. Give them each a sample of your product, and then schedule a time to capture their impressions, if not right away!

Chapter 9

BEFORE AND AFTERS

I am only going to take a moment to touch on this topic. It does not apply to everyone, but for those to whom it does apply, pay attention! This is sales success in a literal snapshot!

When the formerly 250 pound Susie steps in front of the lens at 130 pounds, people are riveted to the screen. When Jane, a severe acne victim, shows her youthful baby-like face next to the worst outbreak she ever had, anyone with pimples cannot look away and wants to know how she did it.

When Debbie shows an image of a severely wrinkled shirt next to the perfect, smooth cloth of that same shirt moments after using her steamer, multitudes of people trapped in garments from the bottom of their laundry basket rejoice. Before and after (B/A) images require very little verbiage to make a huge impact. They are a way of getting a powerful message across at a glance. That message says "this product will get you from the left side of your screen to the right in a blink." Now imagine showing five or more B/As in rapid succession to visually drive-home the point that the results shown are common ones. It is a recipe for sales success. I have sat in the director's chair a thousand times and watched the phone lines spike when compelling B/As are shown one after the other.

Phone lines spike when compelling B/As are shown one after the other.

The B/A shows us what we cannot experience in reality. It lapses time from the before to the after, keeping us from experiencing the process of improvement. It is that often drawn-out process that blunts our excitement. We live in an instant gratification society. Slow doesn't work for us. Imagine if your next diet was a magic pill. How excited would you be swallow it? What if you were 100 pounds overweight, you swallowed a pill and by the time you turned to the mirror, you had a beach body. Sounds pretty good, right? The heck with all the grueling months of watching the weight slowly melt away while eating rabbit fodder and drowning in sweat! Give it to me now! A proper B/A subconsciously shows its viewer that exact thing. It says that the person on the left and the person on the right are the same. You can relate to the struggles of the left side of the screen and have dreamt of the results on the right. The only difference is the product—that thin little line down the middle of the screen. You don't have to suffer through the process. Time is not an issue. In that picture, it doesn't exist. Just the results do and the emotions that go with them.

Of course, consumers are not dumb. You are not "pulling one over" on them. They know there is a process. They acknowledge the need for commitment to it. But, the B/A shows them that it is worth it and mentally shrinks that commitment until it seems far less important and time consuming in light of the results.

Not every product is right for B/A images. I cannot think of a good way to create a B/A image for a battery or an air freshener. However, I am suggesting just one more tool in your belt. If you can find a compelling way to incorporate B/As into your presentation, you should. It can make all the difference in escalating marginal sales to a grand slam!

Chapter 10

THE CTA

There are a few lines that pop to mind when the average person thinks of the classic infomercial:

"Pick up your phone!"

"Don't wait!"

"Call now!"

"Dial that number on the screen!"

These phrases have been recycled in just about every successful infomercial since the mid 1980s. Why? Because without those lines, many people would not grab their credit card and head to the phone. It sounds a bit ridiculous, doesn't it? Tell people what to do and then watch them do it? Heck, I'm still looking for that kind of reaction in my own children and two of them are teenagers! I have to ask them to follow a direction four or five times (if I'm lucky) before they'll commit to doing it! But in the world of product sales, it is a known truth with seasoned presenters. You must ask for the money. You must give the customer a responsive action and short time-line to do it. Most people will simply not decide unless you create circumstances that demand a decision. It is the entire reasoning for that little counter at the bottom of the screen showing how many gizmos are left to sell. There is an art to doing this effectively—keeping the buying experience positive and low-stress for the customer while balancing the inherent urgency of the CTA.

When I script a presentation (and I have scripted hundreds), I must leave time for the host to look at the camera, get matter-of-fact with the viewer and ask them to take out their wallet. It is a delicate moment that must be approached from the right angle. The host is asking the viewer for her trust with one of her most valuable assets—her cash. The appeal must be sensitive, but founded on strong reasoning that makes it easy to see the host's point of view that, "Now is the time to buy, not later." This appeal is known as the call-to-action or CTA. It is verbiage meant to close the sale. In the world of television retail, the CTA is delivered exclusively by the host (not the product guest). It consists of the item number, price, a mention of any discounts being offered and updates on quantities left to sell. A good host will incorporate these elements into a conversational smattering of benefit-rich reasons the viewer should order now. For example, let's look at a vacuum I just launched this morning. I was working with one of the best hosts when it comes to the CTA:

Cory: ". . . and that's why you want this vacuum!"

Host (CTA, to the camera, addressing the viewer):
"Exactly. Look, the price is unbelievable for this kind of power. At 1,000 watts, it has as much suction as a full-sized upright, but it only weighs three lbs and converts to a handheld vac as well! The item number is 456–789, and at $69.95, you just can't find features like this with this kind of manufacturing quality. We're paying the shipping and if you have a major credit card, we'll break up the cost into 3 equal payments over the next 3 months. There is no reason to wait. We don't expect these to last. We've already sold through more than half of our inventory in the past 10 minutes and have hundreds of callers on the lines right now. If you struggle with keeping your house clean, it's probably because you don't have the right tools to save time and get the job done right the first time. That's where this vacuum comes in. Okay, Cory, what's next?"

Cory: "I want to show you how powerful . . ."

If you are selling on TV, a solid CTA should be delivered every 4–5 minutes or so. If you have a long presentation (15 minutes or more), the time between CTAs should decrease as the presentation moves forward. Much like television commercials during a great show, the CTAs should build in frequency as you near the end of the presentation. This creates urgency. Viewers feel compelled not to miss out. If your first CTA was six minutes into a 20 minute presentation, the CTAs should be four minutes apart after minute 15. You need to plan time for your host to deliver them. If you are creating a hosted internet sales video, a CTA should be right at the end of the presentation, wrapping things up. From the aisles of product conventions to national retail television, there is one rule that every good host and guest know—you must ask people to reach into their purse or pocket, pull out their wallet, remove their money and buy. You must deliver the reasons why in short-order and in close proximity to a mention of the price. It may seem ridiculous and simple, but it is a universal truth. Unless you ask people for their money, half of them won't buy.

Activity

Are you selling on TV or on the internet? What kind of video are you creating? If you are selling on TV, ask you network contact how many minutes you will have for your presentation. Then, subtract 25% of your total presentation time to allow for CTAs by your host. If your presentation is 20 minutes, at least 5 minutes should be appropriated for CTAs to close the sale.

If you are selling via internet video, Your CTA can be delivered briefly by your presenter or by text at the close of the video. Take some time now to script a sentence or two and see what your call-to-action will look like. A video for internet should not exceed four to five minutes (more on that later), so be brief but compelling!

_____

_____

_____

_____

_____

_____

_____

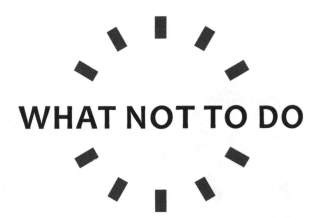

WHAT NOT TO DO

Chapter 11

THE SUBCONSCIOUS MESSAGE

It was a set-up. It *must* have been a set-up. No one would put me on the air with this product, this host, this producer and expect things to hold together. I am holding on by a thread. The hilarity is so thinly covered by my professionalism that my eyes are watering as I stifle myself. One side of me is ready to explode with that laughter that leaves you crying and gasping for air, the other side of me is straining to hold it all back and maintain my composure in front of the lenses. So far, I have hung in there. I have no idea how long it will last—minutes, maybe seconds. I blot another welling tear from my eye while the camera is looking elsewhere.

When the vendor told me the name of the new product he wanted me to present, I said, "Excuse me?" He replied in a louder, slower tone, "The Crevice Stopper." With a chuckle, I asked "What does it do?" He replied with absolute seriousness that it is a stretchy fabric pillow you shove down into the gap between your car seat and center console to keep change, keys, etc...from falling down into the crack." A cool concept and certainly useful, but couldn't he come up with a better name?

When the day came to air it, I learned that my host was Carol. This is when I began to suspect a set-up. Carol has been a professional comedian for most of her life. She is one of the funniest women I have ever met. Our meeting went much as I expected.

Me: "So, Carol, we're selling something new today?"

Carol: "Yeah, I saw—is this right? What's it called? The Crack Stuffer?"

Me: (With a reserved laugh) "No it's the Crevice Stopper."

Carol: "Same thing. What does it do?"

Me: "You push it down into the gap between your car seat and center console to stop change, keys, basically stuff in your pockets from falling down there."

Carol: "And it's a two-pack for 15 dollars? That's a good deal. So what does this crack or, uh, crevice thingy look like?" (I produced one from inside my backpack).Oh, you've got to be kidding me! They used the word crevice in the title and it looks like that? Oh my God! Now, that's funny!"

The product I had just pulled out of my pack was a black, squishy, cylindrical pillow about 12 inches long and two inches in diameter. Even without its title, what I held in my hand looked unmistakably phallic. Carol is a master of spreading hilarity without sharing more than a grin on her own face. I stood there as Carol herself gave in to laughter and knew I was in trouble.

After my host meeting, I met with my producer, Harold. Once again, my set-up meter was pinned in the red. Harold is your classic funny guy. A favorite among the network crews for his quick witted remarks and dead-accurate impersonations, his voice would be in my little earpiece throughout the presentation. Dear God.

Harold: "Hey, Cory. Did you meet with Carol?"

Me: "Yeah, just now."

Harold: "And?"

He was fishing for how things went. He had seen the product and the title. That would be part of his preparations for the show.

Me: "She thinks it's a great deal and likes what it does."

Harold (leaning in): "And?!"

Me: "It's going to be interesting."

Harold (Leaning back with a belly laugh) "You can say that again!"

By the time we had finished our meeting, I started planning on watching the end of Old Yeller or the opening scene from Saving Private Ryan—anything to depress me. There was no way I was going to make it through this with a straight face. It just wouldn't be good form to let the nation know how hysterical I thought this product was. And I knew that I could not foresee all the ways this could go sideways once I was into the presentation.

An hour later, I stood on the outdoor set waiting for Carol to arrive. She was being pushed in a wheel chair by a runner from the indoor Studio to Studio O (for outdoors), a 200 yard sprint through the network halls. We were in a commercial break. Carol had 2 minutes to make it onto the outdoor set and 5" heels are not overly conducive to running. As she stepped from her wheelchair, she clapped her hands together and said "Ok, where's Cory? Let's sell the Crack Stuffer!" I reminded her that it was called the "Crevice Stopper". She replied, "Same thing," then turned to the camera and welcomed the TV viewers to our outdoor set and our next item.

Those first few minutes took everything I had to keep my composure. I have to thank Harold, my producer, for not torturing me. Instead, I heard stories afterward that he had been breathing in Carol's earpiece and she performed various suggestive hand motions with my product. At one point, the camera was on my ISO shot (a shot of just me as I talk to the viewer). Just outside of the camera's view, Carol was holding the pillow at waist height and swinging it from side to side, around in circles and smacking it on the edge of the tabletop in front of us. All of this was in my peripheral vision as I looked into the lens and talked to the nation. No matter how hard I tried not to, everything I said was the wrong thing:

"It fits deep into your crack."

"It's a tight fit so nothing else can go down there."

"Just shove it down into your gap and let it do its job."

There did not seem to be a safe way to describe it! Every time I opened my mouth it got worse! I had to stop speaking a few times to choke back my laughter. I must have sounded strangely staccato. Finally, Harold told us to move on to the car demo. Carol interrupted my shaky verbiage to say "Cory, didn't you want to show us something in the car?" I stopped mid sentence and said "Yes, let's do that." Then, I marched over to the car, taking advantage of the few moments of respite to gather myself. Carol told the customer the item number and price of the Crevice Stopper, then tossed back over to me, now sitting in a convertible ready to demonstrate.

I showed the little pillow to the camera and pointed out a specific feature.

"About 3/4 of the way down your Crevice Stopper is a small slit that goes all the way through the pillow. This is for your seatbelt connector to pass through as you install it. Let me show you."

Since the pillow was made of stretchy material, this little three-inch slit was tough to see unless something opened it up. I shoved my pointer and middle finger into the slit, keeping them straight and parted them, wiggling them around to show off the opening. From behind the pillow, this seemed a perfectly natural way to show the customer what I meant. However, I glanced over at the on-set monitors showing me the camera's point of view. What I saw made me catch my breath. It appeared so suggestive, I was mortified! I instantly pulled my fingers back out of the slit and started laughing. It took me a few moments to barely pull myself together and move on to the rest of the demonstration.

Now, I sit here in this car after describing how deep and tight the Crevice Stopper fits into the crack and am counting the moments until the presentation ends. The thread I am using to secure my composure is invisibly thin, frayed, stretched taught and desperately anxious to snap. I step from the vehicle and return to the table. Carol sees the inevitability of my condition and rescues me like the true comic professional she is. With barely a grin, she repeats how the Crevice Stopper works, who it can benefit, gives the item number and price and closes the sell. I close my eyes and exhale in relief, letting the laughter surface.

The above account is not fabricated. Everything you read actually happened and if I had to devote an entire book to such stories, I could. The viewer has no idea what actually happens in the background or just out of the camera's view. It is an exciting, emotionally charged environment full of expressive, outgoing people. There is never a dull moment.

In retrospect, I think I did quite well selling the Crack—I mean, Crevice Stopper. I watched a recording of the presentation later and my composure was convincing. There were only a few moments where I could tell something was up. I was glad. I held on by shear focus and willpower. Regardless, I have an entire group of friends who never miss an opportunity to poke some fun using the words "crack or crevice" with a grin.

It is an exciting, emotionally charged environment full of expressive, outgoing people.

I told this story because it is a prime example of one specific facet when crafting a product presentation. What your viewers don't see and what remains unsaid is just as powerful as what they do see and what you do say. There is a subconscious message constantly being relayed to your viewer and he/she is extremely sensitive to it. Your job is to foresee these messages and steer them in the direction you wish to head. Unfortunately, for the inventor of the Crevice Stopper, he sabotaged his own presentation with a product title and appearance that sent a very strong suggestive message, and he did not even realize it! Think about what your viewer might infer from your product, presenter or presentation and craft it accordingly.

For example, I have sold many fans and air conditioners. I have also sold many heaters. When I am planning to walk on-air to sell something that cools you off, I reach for a blue shirt. When I am selling something that heats you up, I wear red, burgundy or a sweater, regardless of how hot or cold the studio is! This may seem like an insignificant nuance, but believe me, it is not! Your viewer will respond to what they feel coming through their screen. If you look warm and they are cold, they will want what you have.

Retailers everywhere pull out their Christmas cheer as early as October to inspire gift-giving. In this consumer-driven world, it is tough to resist that electronic gizmo with wreaths on walls and bells in the background music. It sends a message. It says, "The time is upon you. Time to buy stuff for everyone else as well!"

You must, of course, measure this concept with a dose of reality. I once saw a guest walk on air to sell a windshield cover that kept ice from freezing to your window. He was wearing a parka. Unfortunately for him, it was March in Florida, the network was trying to blow out the last of their inventory at the end of the season, it was 80 degrees and his host was in a summer dress. It looked ridiculous. He walked off-air soaked in sweat and had to peel of his jacket. The only message he was sending was that he was desperately trying to send a message!

Do your best to measure the little things in your presentation that might help you relay a good message without saying it and try to foresee the nuances that might undermine your sales efforts. Sometimes, that unspoken message can cause just as much of a reaction in your viewer as what they hear!

Activity

What is the nature of your product? Write six adjectives below to describe it.

1. _____

2. _____

3. _____

4. _____

5. _____

6. _____

Now, consider your subconscious messaging. If you reflect on the six adjectives above, what elements should be in place during the presentation to send that message? Jot down some ideas.

1. _____

2. _____

3. _____

4. _____

5. _____

6. _____

Chapter 12

WINGING IT

Andy was a master of improvisation. Even now, in this situation, he wasn't sweating. He knew he'd think of something. Heck, he had been in thousands of crazy situations before. If there was adventure involved, he was always in. His buddies and he had built a speedboat out of some boards, roofing tar and an old Chevy engine. It worked great until they took off at night and accidentally had the water-ski tow-rope tied to the dock. It ripped the whole backside of the boat off and sunk it to the bottom of the lake. Even then, he bobbed in the water laughing it off and moved on to the next big adventure.

One time Andy skied black diamond runs with boards taped to his feet instead of real skis. Another time he accidently set his high school's lawn on fire and managed to walk away innocent. His mother's hair went grey early.

After getting his pilot's license, he flew an airplane with an old wooden prop that snapped its tip off while flying. Being unbalanced, it shook the rivets out of the plane! He killed the engine, glided it into a farmer's field, borrowed a saw, cut the other side of the prop even with the side that broke, gunned the engine and flew home. The farmer thought he was insane! He once chased his small plane down a runway after it got stuck in a pothole and he had climbed out to push. He barely caught up with it just before it went off the end of the runway. He climbed into the cockpit to the sound of howling laughter coming over the radio from the control tower. Then there was the time he overloaded his plane with a cargo of bomb fuses and shot down a runway that ended in a cliff, hoping that he would remain in the air when the ground ran out! His little craft slowly lumbered back up after a shocking plummet. He got the cargo to its destination on time. Yes, Andy had been through quite a few scrapes. This would be no different.

His plane was in the air, the storm outside was raging, but he knew these mountains well and he would make it back. Although storms in this region could be severe, he hadn't bothered delaying his plan to fly home or even double check the forecast. He was a good pilot and knew his plane well. He was immensely confident and this was just another adventure. For a New England pilot, winter storms are the worst. Planes fly better when they're not frozen. Andy had his instruments and knew to trust them. He was no rookie. The airport was not much further.

As he flew over the Otis reservoir, he glanced out the window. He was low enough that even in this storm, he might be able to see the lights from the turnpike off to his right. No such luck. It was utter blackness and howling wind. His plane lurched harder than usual as the wind slammed into it, bringing with it the ticking sound of hail. This was bad. Hail could be downright dangerous to a small craft. He would like to have gotten above or around this storm, but home was only a little way off and he needed to decrease his altitude in preparation for landing.

Just then, then needle on his VHF gauge dropped limply to the bottom of the instrument. It had lost signal. He waited a few seconds for it to respond, but nothing happened. This was his homing gauge it kept him on track as he flew into the airport. He no longer had any heading to fly on. He decided to circle and see if he could get the gauge to come back to life. He leveled out, turned the yoke to the left and began banking widely, his eyes riveted to the meter.

2 hours later, Andy was still circling. His gauge never responded. The storm had increased in violence. His radio communication with the airport tower was now intermittent. Ice had been forming on his wings and he was losing altitude. He had grown up in these mountains. He knew that the peaks around him were now further off the ground than he was and he was flying utterly blind. His fuel was running dangerously low and he had finally started to sweat. If he pulled out of his circle in an attempt to fly out of the storm, he could collide with a mountain at any moment. It seemed inevitable. He was going down.

The best he could hope for was to circle low enough that he would see some street lights and use them to find a place to land. He pushed his talk button and spoke into his microphone:

"Mayday, Mayday. This is Cessna flight 217 out of Boston. I am going down. I repeat, I am going down. If you are looking for the wreckage, it will be in that vicinity of the Otis reservoir and the Massachusetts Turnpike."

Andy repeated this message three times, and then released his talk button. He glanced nervously at the VHF gauge, then his fuel gauge and altimeter. He was out of time. He took a deep breath and pushed the yoke forward, dropping the airplane's nose toward the ground, wishing he had relied on more than his wits to get him home.

Five years ago, I watched a guest walk onto national television to represent his product, a method for trash disposal that was completely green. He was the inventor of the product and knew everything that could be known about it, but he had not planned out his presentation and was obviously counting on his knowledge alone for his product's success. He had sunk every dime his family had into coming up with the inventory for the presentations. He had flown in from Montana, was paying for his stay with his own funds and was scheduled for three airings.

When he went on air, he jumped right into a list of his product's features. You could tell he had been to a hundred trade shows, but this was no trade show. Although he had an air of confidence about him, his presentation floundered about without any real direction. He gave a list of things his product could do, but did have any strong initial statement or emotional angle to grab his viewer's attention. The phone lines quickly dwindled. His presentation was cut from 10 minutes to 6 and he walked off air feeling defeated. He was projected to sell hundreds and hundreds of his product. He sold less than 50. The remainders of his airings were cancelled due to poor performance and he flew home. His inventory was returned back to him.

The nature of television retail is unforgiving. In my experience, I have less than a minute after I am introduced on-air to emotionally engage my viewer and give them a solid reason to keep watching. A product must show its viability within one or two airings or it will get the ax. The nature of internet video is even more unforgiving. According to research by Visible Measures, 20% of viewers will click away from an online marketing video in 10 seconds or fewer. We judge other people harshest of all. According to Forbes, we have seven precious seconds to create a first impression! Imagine, within seven seconds your viewer will decide if they like you and trust you or not! So why would you ever present a product, pick your presenter or create a product demonstration video without a well planned and rehearsed strategy? Don't waste any of those precious minutes in the spotlight, especially the first few seconds! They are too valuable to flounder! You must have direction and a presentation plan

Captain Jack Sparrow had a compass. Dora the Explorer has a map. Iron man has—well, a super computer with undoubtedly the most sophisticated GPS ever conceived.

The point is that we all know instinctively, if you want to get from point A to B for the first time, you must plan your route. You need some directions or a roadmap. In the world of television and video, you want to get from "Hello, I'm John," to "Thanks for buying!" How are you going to get your viewers from A to B? First, you need to know who your viewer is. What do they do with their days? How do they think? How do you think when you dig into your experiences and stand in your viewer's shoes? Then, you need a solid presentation plan You need a map to lead yourself and your crew through the mess of possibilities and to that goal where the viewer clicks, "Buy!"

By the way, Andy made it out of his predicament. On his final circle, low to the ground and bracing for impact, his VHF gauge finally twitched. He said a quick prayer, turned his wheel into the direction of that twitch and flew right between two mountain peaks, out of the raging storm and directly over the runway of his home-town airport. I am personally very glad he made it. He would later father a son named Cory.

(Note: Later on in this book, we will look at storyboarding your product's presentation. It is too early to approach that just yet, but don't worry. I will give you an activity later on be ensure you don't "wing it!")

Chapter 13

OVERCOMPLICATING

Your do not want to play Scrabble with me. I have been grinningly prodded by every friend I have ever had for the way I describe things. My wife and kids are no exception. My nine and ten-year-olds will stare and nod. My 15-year-old daughter will say "Huh?" then tell me she has no idea what I am saying. My supremely intellectual 17-year-old son will slap me on the back and say, "Good one, Dad," and then provide me with variations of the same word. My wife will smile at me and tell me I could have said the same thing much simpler. Simple verbiage does not come easy for me. I grew up with a man who was also an intellectual. He studied scripture and ancient texts. He read Greek. His favorite pastor was not just a theologian, but also a philosopher and linguist. He adored history and devoured volumes of it. He revered the writings of great minds and immersed himself in

Shakespeare for recreation. His own interpretations of the world were weighted with the wisdom of countless geniuses. When he was serious and his mouth opened, it was worth earnest attention. The everyday exchanges in our home were evidence of my father's influence. To this day, if you speak with any one of my four siblings, they speak the same as I do.

I recently sat down with a prestigious and very highly paid talent trainer from Manhattan. She told me when you are speaking to a television retail consumer, you need to imagine your customer has no prior knowledge of your product or its technology. Close your eyes and imagine your child at age 6, now open your eyes and explain your product. Although this may or may not be an exaggeration, the message is clear and true. The nature of video is that it spoon-feeds you. It requires very little effort on the viewer's part. When someone pulls up a video online or clicks on their TV, they are not expecting to have to work. They want simple! Also, realize that your viewer is not sitting on the edge of her seat, hanging on every word. You need to assume her eyes are glazed over because it is 2 AM and she has been surfing the web for hours. She has had her television on low volume in the background for most of the day and is walking through the room to put laundry away, stopping for a quick glance at the screen. She is not seeking a PHD on your product. She wants to know that it works and why it is better than her other options.

Each year, I do my best to participate in "The Great American Teach In" at my kid's school. I have to stand up in front of the class, tell them what I do for a living and give them a chance to participate somehow. Two years ago, I brought in the Xbox. I was a hit! To this day, I walk the elementary school halls and kids I don't even know high-five me as I walk by. I am a total celebrity! However, I was not just there to let them take turns with a game system. I was there to show them what I do. I picked four kids to write down a few reasons someone would want to buy the Xbox, and then present them in front of the class. Afterward, I took a turn speaking to them. It was amazing to hear what a bunch of third graders thought. They said things like "The Xbox is the best game system there is. It looks better on your TV than other ones do. You don't need any remotes to play. You can play with lots of people all together." This is what they understand. If a mom was walking through a room with arms full of laundry and she was in the market for a game console, any one of those kid's statements would have grabbed her. If a web-surfer was staring with red eyes at their monitor at 3am and they heard any one of those kid's statements, they would get it right away.

Simplifying my speech has been an ongoing training exercise for me. I have had to embrace less-descriptive verbiage simply because it is easier to understand. There is something inside me that pushes back when a perfectly enlightening word is replaced with one a bit less potent. But, that is how people speak to each other and a product presentation is an easy conversation, not a professorial lecture.

Other than speech, there are several pitfalls to watch out for when creating your presentation. These elements are sure indicators that you are overcomplicating.

1. Abbreviations and Acronyms

"Excuse me, sir. Seeing as how the VP is such a VIP, shouldn't we keep the PC on the QT? 'Cause if it leaks to the VC he could end up MIA, and then we'd all be put on KP."

**—Robin Williams as Adrian Cronauer,
Good Morning Vietnam**

Unless they are common tongue like NASA, LOL, PHD, ASAP, or similarly familiar acronyms, do not use abbreviations and assume your viewer knows what you mean. You are more than likely confusing them and they are losing interest in listening to you!

2. Industry Terms

Steve Rogers: "Does Loki need any particular kind of power source?"

Bruce Banner: "He's got to heat the cube to 120,000,000 Kelvin just to break through the Coulomb barrier."

Tony Stark: "Unless, Selvig has figured out how to stabilize the quantum tunneling effect."

Bruce Banner: "Well, if he could do that he could achieve Heavy Ion Fusion at any reactor on the planet."

Tony Stark: "Finally, someone who speaks English!"

Steve Rogers: "Is that what just happened?"

In the above scene from the 2012 hit movie, The Avengers, Steve Rogers (Captain America) is utterly lost. He is not a scientist like Tony Stark (Iron Man) or Bruce Banner (the Hulk). He is a simple kid with lots of heart and some superhuman abilities. If you take away the superhuman part and more than half his age, Steve Rogers is your product's audience! You need to keep him in the loop, engaged in the conversation. Keep your terminology easy to understand.

I like to call it the "billboard approach." When you are driving down the highway and you spot a billboard, you only have a few seconds to take in the entire message and understand it. If it takes a traffic jam to give you the time to read and comprehend it, then it is wasted advertising. Take the billboard approach with your verbiage. Take industry concepts and make them easy to understand, zipping by at 70 miles per hour. If only the people in your industry would understand exactly what you mean, then you are ensuring a loss of sales. You are not showing off your knowledge to your customer. You are making them mentally tune out!

3. Requiring Too Much Imagination

From time to time, I work with a product vendor who is very passionate about a certain aspect of their product which is difficult to explain and often there is no budget to create support materials to help relate the concept to the viewer. This can be very challenging. Sometimes, as critical as that point is, it is better to omit the product feature all together, rather than risk an explanation. Explanations of this sort can end up a tangled mess, no matter how thoroughly you script them ahead of time.

One of the things I am paid for is my ability to take complex concepts and relate them simply to my viewer. However, what if the primary differentiating factor of an air conditioner is that it has a brand new technology designed to mist water onto the A/C condenser and through rapid evaporation, and cool that condenser allowing for a faster reduction in room temperature than other A/Cs can provide? I cannot simply say that my A/C is more powerful and cools faster than others. My customer would expect to hear that from every A/C company out there! I must deliver a reason that makes sense and substantiates my claim—not to mention a reason why they must continually fill a water reservoir to keep the A/C operating at maximum potential!

**Take complex concepts and
relate them simply to the viewer.**

This is where support elements come in. If your statement cannot deliver your meaning simply, you need to acquire photo, video or animation support to help explain the concept. Lucky for me, the A/C I am referring to above was one I sold and had great animation support showing a simple breakdown of the A/C's interior where the magic took place. As I spoke to the concept, the animation relayed my statements visually, making the feature easy to grasp.

Getting tangled up in complex explanations that require lots of imagination from your viewer will not only make their eyes glaze over, it will eat up super-precious time!

4. Difficult Demos

"Demonstrations" is a very broad topic which I will delve into later in this book in far more detail. However, for the sake of this chapter, let me speak to those demos which should be avoided due to being overly complicated.

In my first year as a product presenter, I sold a cleaning spray that was very powerful yet harmless to the environment in your home. Unlike other cleaners, which release potent and harmful chemicals into the air each time they are used, my cleaner was completely free of any toxins or harmful chemicals and fumes. It actually reduced harmful gases that might still be in the air from other cleaners! The vendor and I partnered together to create a demonstration that would show this.

We constructed two Plexiglas boxes. Inside each box was a laboratory instrument called a VOC (Volatile Organic Compounds) meter. VOCs are airborne contaminants that are unhealthy to breathe and are released into your home from the off-gassing of new carpet, paint, glue, cleaners, etc. Into one box, I sprayed a common glass cleaner and into the other box, I sprayed my cleaner. The glass cleaner caused the VOC meter to spike. My cleaner did not cause the meter to raise even a single digit. Then came the real impactful part. I sprayed my cleaner into the box used for the glass cleaner. The meter in that box plummeted back down, showing that my cleaner actually counter-acted the harmful chemicals produced by the glass cleaner! I anticipated a home-run in sales following that demo. It certainly differentiated my product from others. When it came time to present my cleaner on national television, I executed the demonstration perfectly. I also watched the phone lines out of the corner of my eye (there is a monitor in the studio that shows me how many people are calling to order). The call volume dropped lower and lower and lower. After my demo, I had almost no interest from the viewers. Their eyes had glazed over and they had tuned out. I had also consumed more than half of my time on-air with just one demo. I used the remaining time I had to bounce from one dirty item to another, cleaning like wildfire! I cleaned a stove top, jewelry, a hubcap, a window, a sink, grease, ink, nail polish and marker. The phone lines jumped to life. By the end of the presentation, we had hundreds of bottles sold. I did not meet sales projections, but I did resurrect interest in my product with quick, impactful demos showing my cleaner in action.

Demonstrations should be quick and easy to understand. They should almost speak for themselves without your talent explaining them. When a woman walks by her volume-less TV with her laundry basket or a trade-show attendee strolls past your booth in the din of a packed aisle, the demo they see on screen should rivet them at a glance!

Demonstrations should be
quick and easy to understand.

---

5. Over-planning

Think of how you planned errands when you were a teenager and how you plan them now as an adult. As a teenager, you thought you could get six errands done in 90 minutes, 15 minutes apiece. (Never worked did it?) Now, as an adult, you know that driving time is always slower than you plan and the line in the store will always be longer than you think. You may need time for incoming cell calls and you give yourself a 20 minute buffer just in case. You now plan three errands in 90 minutes and it usually works out. It is the same thing with a product presentation. You cannot expect to unload everything you know about your product and you cannot be unrealistic with your timing. Everything will take longer than you think and time streaks by. Always have a repeatable demo or some key points in your back pocket in case you run short, but they are just contingencies. Chances are, you will be surprised at how fast time goes by. You do not want to get caught up in a hundred points and a dozen demos, and then hear the buzzer! Do not hit the end of your clock and realize you haven't done your product justice!

In the world of television retail, each product is planned for a certain amount of air time. The clock starts. By the time your host finishes her introduction of the product and you, two minutes has passed. The host will interject to ask questions. Some may derail you from the direction you were headed and you will have to circle back around. Depending on your host, he/she will close the sale (call-to-action for the viewer to buy now) every few minutes. Each time, it will eat up another minute, sometimes more. If you are planned to have 12 minutes on air, you need to plan on having a maximum of 8 minutes of sales time! The same will happen when creating a product video for the internet. You will have far less time to engage your viewer and execute your entire presentation than a television network would give you. Plan simply!

Activity

List some potentially confusing or overly-complicated elements in your presentation. Convert them into easily understood, simplified elements.

Confusing		Easily Understood
	➡	
	➡	
	➡	
	➡	
	➡	

Chapter 14

FEAR FACTOR

Shortly after moving into our home, Elizabeth and I were laying in bed, having committed to a much deserved mid-Saturday nap. Our bedroom fan whirred in the corner (we sleep with one for white noise), and after a long work week, our eyes slammed shut and the world blacked out. We had hours ahead of us. Our children were out of the house, all four of them staying with friends. It was a rare day. About 15 minutes into our nap, I awoke. Elizabeth hadn't stirred. The first thing I wondered after turning to my bedside clock was *Why on earth am I awake?* It took a few seconds for my brain to process that question. Then I noticed it—the smell in the air. Something did not smell right to me. Although faint, the smell was potent enough that it brought me back from the abyss I had plummeted into. I turned and gently woke Elizabeth.

"Baby, do you smell something?"

"What? Huh? Cory, I was asleep," she whimpered.

"Something is not right," I said.

"Sweetheart, go back to sleep. It's nothing," she replied.

I laid my head back down. I continued to sniff the air.

On the other side of our home reside our teenagers. Their bedrooms are as far from my bed as you can be without stepping outside the walls of our house. In the hall ceiling, between their bedrooms, lies an A/C return vent. It continually cools air by pulling it up into the air handler, and then re-circulating it back into all the rooms in the house. At that moment, It was recirculation to our entire home the wisps of white smoke that were curling up from under my 17-year old's bedroom door. After being diluted into all the rooms of our house, only the faintest odor had reached my nose, but it was enough and I thank God that I awoke.

I sat up in my bed, and disturbed Elizabeth once again, who whined pleadingly.

"I can't sleep. I have to go see what I smell. We are alone in the house. This is not right," I said. She groaned.

I wrapped a blanket around myself and walked to our bedroom door, pulling it open. A stronger odor struck my nose. I followed it across the living room, to the right through our kitchen and across the dining room. By now, I had begun to perceive a slight white haze hanging in the air, more so toward the ceiling. My adrenaline began to kick-in as my steps became more purposeful. As I entered the hall leading to our teenager's bedrooms, I saw the smoke coming from under my son's door. I knew enough not to throw it open. I listened intently for a moment. I felt the door with the back of my hand, then the doorknob. Both were cool. I slowly turned the knob and opened the door. Choking, toxic smoke billowed out at the top of the doorway into the hall. The was no evidence of fire, but the smoke and fumes were suffocating. I held my breath crouched low and crossed the room to the windows, threw both of them wide open, and put my son's fan onto the sill, hoping to blow the smoke into the backyard. In a minute or so, the air had cleared enough for me to see. Still crouching below the lingering smog, I discovered the source, ripped the plug out of the wall, and tossed it out the window into the yard.

My son had a pet tortoise. He had constructed a habitat for "Rose" on his floor out of plywood, sand, and a small reptile lagoon. Being a desert tortoise, Rose required bright sunlight for health. Dominick was using a work lamp with a large clip on it to suspend a UV light above Rose's habitat. The clip had failed. The lamp had slowly descended from its perch until it sat bulb-down under its aluminum dome against the plywood. When I finally discovered it, it had burned a six-inch hole through 3/4 of an inch of plywood as well as the carpet and foam under the habitat and was baking the concrete foundation of our house. Rose had retreated to the far corner of her habitat and was actively trying to drag her shell up the wall. The plywood and carpet were smoldering with traces of red embers and were surrounded by a large black ring of charcoal. I am very thankful that homes these days are mostly made of fire-retardant materials.

40 years ago, I might have awakened to flames consuming half my house!

All of this took place because we had not replaced the old, dysfunctional smoke detectors that hung dead from our ceilings. We had moved in a few months previous and had not made those detectors a priority, assuming that if they were up there, they must be working.

Smoke detectors. There are tons and tons of statistics and horror stories about people who neglected to have them. My wife is a certified EMT/firefighter. She hasn't practiced in years, but knows the value of early fire detection and has seen the lack of it. Our household, more than most, knows that we need a good system in place to warn us if a fire begins. Shame on us for not listening to our own wisdom. We now have great detectors—detectors made by the biggest name in the industry and ones that I sold on national television!

I had a powerful story to tell. Not only was my wife an EMT/ Firefighter and had lots of input on the importance of good detectors, but the story I just related to you gave me personal experience regarding the lack of proper foresight and prevention. When I stepped out onto the air and my image was broadcast into over 150 million households, I did not tell that story the way you just heard it. I knew that scaring people was not how you convince the masses. A few would buy, but not nearly the number that would if I focused on the advantages. I focused on the feelings of safety and security, on the benefits of early warning and the importance of loved ones in your home. I related my story quickly so I would not lead people down a dark, depressing path, but simply bring some credibility to my opinions on the product. You need to do the same.

"Fear Factor" does not sell. Instinctively, most people think it will. Many think that we can scare people into buying a product, but people do not buy fear. When you sell something on "Fear Factor," you are telling people that having your product in their home will continually remind them of the horror stories they want to avoid. You are selling them stress and worry. Would you pursue stress and worry yourself? No! You would run from it, and so do your customers. They instinctively find a justification to walk away. Remember that the heart decides, and then the brain finds a justification for what the heart feels. When a person is hit with a "Fear Factor" presentation, his heart wants to run away. It is just a small matter of time before his brain will find a reason why his heart can have what it wants.

People do not buy fear.

If you spend most of your time on the looming darkness of the problem and not the bright promise of the solution, and if you hand your customer bad feelings they would avoid if they could, you will only see their backs as they retreat from you. Keep things positive and uplifting. Give people security, peace of mind, a feeling of accomplishment, the hope for beauty or the benefits of a great solution. That is what people will look forward to having as a part of their lives and will pay to have it!

Activity

Did you have a "fear factor" presentation in mind when you first imagined your product on video or TV? If so, look back at your benefits and Key Points. Flip each fear-filled message into one that is uplifting.

Fear Factor Benefit or Key Point		Uplifting New Message
	➡	
	➡	
	➡	
	➡	
	➡	

Chapter 15

NEGATIVE VOCABULARY

I spent almost two years of my life as a stay-at-home dad. Elizabeth asked if I would step down from my career as a television director, move our family to Nashville and support her in pursuing a singing career. I agreed and was thus initiated into the small circle of men who genuflect in front of most moms. I had no idea how far that decision would push me physically, emotionally and psychologically. I took over raising my youngest son at four months old. I was also juggling a 1 ½ year old boy, six year old girl and eight year boy. After a few weeks, I felt as though half my brain cells had died and I could not speak without sounding like Barney, no matter who I was talking to. Did I mention I was home-schooling the older children? Yup, I decided that

I would over-achieve right from the start. I don't think my children learned anything from me during those first few months. However, they schooled me every single hour of every day. On second thought, that's not entirely accurate. They did learn that dad was a horrible cook and the best part of his day is when mommy came home. No matter how out of control things felt, no matter who was throwing a fit or what question needed an answer, Mommy would sweep in through the door and have the whole house running like a well oiled machine in minutes. Tears were dried, emotions were calmed—and then she would see to the kids.

However, I have always been an ambitious student and I applied myself to my lessons. A year into my home-maker status, I could throw open a sparse pantry, pull out random items, throw a dinner together in 30 minutes without even measuring the seasonings and have the kid asking for seconds. I could change two diapers in two minutes complete with powder and not even a trampoline could make them fall off. I could shop with half the budget and make the groceries last twice as long. I could even find some time to read a book or work on a project between play dates. When the kids got hurt or woke in the night, they would come to my side of the bed rather than Elizabeth's. It took some time but I got it, even though I learned that I'll never be as amazing at it as my wife.

One of the powerful lessons I learned through observing Elizabeth in action was one of phrasing.

If my son Ethan asked for ice cream, I do not say "Absolutely not! Your dinner is in ten minutes!" Instead,

I would say "You bet. Right after dinner, you can have a bowl! We're eating in just a few minutes!" When Danika would ask for a pet kitten, I would not say "Are you kidding! I can't even get you to pick up your dirty clothes! Why would I give you an animal?" Instead, I would say, "I'll tell you what, Dani. Lets look at the ways you can help out around here and if you do a good job, we'll talk about getting you a pet."

When you raise young children, you learn that often the difference between a smile and a meltdown is phrasing. When you present a product, there are always two ways you can frame it. It can be negative or positive. The first will subliminally depress your viewer. The second will inspire them. Framing a concept with uplifting vocabulary and sentence structure is important. If I were selling a $40 item at a sale price of $20, I would not say "I am charging you $20," I would say "I am saving you 20!" If I made a strong point, rather than saying the phrase "When I say this works, I'm not lying!" Instead, I would say "When I say this works, I am absolutely serious!" If I were selling an anti-virus program I would not say "This keeps your computer from crashing," I would say "This keeps you safe and protected!" It is all in the words you choose and how you assemble them. Positive beats negative every time. There will be circumstances when a negative phrase is simply necessary to set the scene for a product. However, the scale should always tip heavily toward the positive.

In the world of live retail television, where everything is completely unscripted, this is an important concept to master. I must sometimes change my verbiage as it comes into my head and a split-second before it comes out of my mouth it to give it a positive spin. I must measure my words on the fly, and make adjustments as needed. Negativity is contagious. It creeps into the minds of your audience and siphons away their enthusiasm. When it is over-used, it is a formula for disaster. Be deliberate in your phrasing. Encourage enthusiasm and let your positive descriptions and feelings overflow into your viewer's living room or office. It could be one of the big reasons they begin to seek out your products specifically. People love to surround themselves with others that uplift them and make them feel good about themselves and their world. You are a part of that. Don't let them down!

Chapter 16

HOW WILL I EVER CHOOSE?

Look in your left hand. There sits a coupon for a set of cookware, $20 off on a set of ten pieces. On the store shelf in front of you sits the box. It looks beautiful. You can imagine using it in your kitchen in place of the mismatched set you assembled over the years—the set with all the non-stick scraped off that eggs stick to so horribly. Just below that box is another set. It is the same price, but offers twelve pieces, one of them, the extra-large frying pan you have always wanted. However, the box with the coupon is made by a well known brand and might last longer. You think: Hmmm, just because the twelve-piece set is not a brand you are familiar with, does not mean it is bad. It could be great. Then again, you usually get what you pay for and the coupon brand would be more expensive without the coupon. It is probably a better quality. Just then, you notice another set on a higher shelf. Sixteen pieces for $20 more. It is a blue porcelain color and would match your kitchen's color scheme perfectly! You told your wife and daughter you would be in and out of the store. They are waiting in the car for you at the curb, engine running. You can feel the weight of time ticking by as they wait. Finally, devoid of any epiphanies, you reach for the coupon box, pull it off the shelf, turn to walk away, see the other set, then put the coupon box back again. You huff and walk out of the store empty handed. You tell yourself, *This is ridiculous. My cookware is just fine. I don't need anything new right now. I can wait a few more months.* You tell your family as much when you get into the car. Your mind just found a way to justify what your heart was feeling—frustration and a desire to get rid of it by logically avoiding the circumstances.

Many, many times I have been asked to sell product configurations that have too many options. Television sales time is short. You must be able to help people understand their options quickly and move into showing the product in action. You must get beyond the variations the customer has to choose from and help them to emotionally engage with the benefits. If it takes too long to describe choices, people's eyes glaze over. Their minds fog. It interrupts the momentum and magic of the presentation and viewers mentally tune-out. It is too much intellectual rigor and viewers don't want to work that hard.

I have consulted with producers, planners, hosts and sales managers many times when this issue arises. With a slight simplification of product offer, I have seen products go from marginal sales to monumental success. I could give you dozens of examples of this pitfall, but I have no desire to make you wade through another paragraph like the one above. Here is a truth that every seasoned product presenter knows: When a customer has trouble making a choice, they opt NOT to choose. They move on.

When a customer has trouble making a choice, they opt NOT to choose. They move on.

It is far better to create two presentations, each with its own simple, distinct product offer, than to try to cram it all into one video segment. Overall, you will lose money if you try. You might save time and money up front. You might eat up less capital hiring a crew and talent for one day rather than two, but ultimately, your sales will suffer and that is the whole reason you are creating your video. You can offer options, but keep them easy to understand: A computer with a choice of the 19" or 21" monitor; a mattress with a choice of twin, queen or king; a blender in silver, black or white. If your customer can understand their choices easily, they are far more likely to buy!

Activity

Do you have a complicated offer? How can you simplify it to make it more palatable for your customer?

Notes: _____

_____

_____

_____

_____

_____

_____

_____

_____

_____

_____

Chapter 17

BASHING THE COMPETITION

In the 2012 presidential race, Barack Obama ran a campaign focused on the celebration of inclusivity. He had to deflect all kinds of negative accusations from his opponent, Mitt Romney and the press. Obama was accused of being a Muslim (a tender topic, especially for the ignorant following 9/11) and not being born in the USA, thus undermining his eligibility for the presidency altogether. You would think that after all of the negativity he had to juggle from the press and his opponent, he would be the last person to throw stones at Romney regarding his faith or social status. However, that's exactly what Obama did. He ran ads that ended with the kicker "Mitt Romney: Not one of us." Wow! Regardless of how you felt about Obama's platform and values, a statement like that only did damage to his campaign. It seems that every four years, we have to sit through this rubbish as it reaches right into our living rooms and makes us take turns disliking each political candidate for the ads they attack their opponent with. In my humble opinion, it only hurts the person throwing the stones and casts a dark cloud over their character. It makes my attention turn in favor of the other candidate.

You must be careful when you craft a presentation that you are not disparaging your competition. It only hurts you. It shows your customer that you must resort to cheap shots because you have nothing better. It appears desperate. It also wounds your character in their eyes. You want your customer to warm up to you, but you are showing them that you are cold and calculating when handling others. You are no longer the guy they want to have over for dinner. You are the neighbor they try to avoid with distant waves and false smiles. Remember, your viewer will decide if they like you or not within seven seconds. They will continue to re-evaluate that first impression continually throughout your presentation. You do not want anything to reflect badly on your character or that of your company!

Your viewer will decide if they like
you or not within seven seconds.

That being said, you can certainly point out what your product can do and that others on the market fall short by comparison. However, it should be a generalized brief statement. It should not point out specific brands, be foundational to your presentation, nor pivotal to your ability to sell your product. Every product on the market has things wrong with it, no matter how premium or pricey. Chances are if you throw stones, your competition has plenty of ways they could throw them right back. No one has created the perfect anything. Even if your gizmo is functionally perfect, it could lack manufacturing quality so you can keep the price down or could cost a bundle to provide both perfect functionality and manufacturing quality. It is always a give and take. No product can have both sides of the scale sore skyward simultaneously. One side must go down as the other goes up.

I once bought a premium car for a bargain and thought I had found great functionality, price and quality all in one package. It felt that way until I blew a headlight and it was going to cost me $1,600 for a replacement! Then, I had to pay $200 for an oil change and basic service. The first time I needed a brake job, it was almost $2,000. I spent over $7,000 in the first 2 years of owning that vehicle just to keep it on the road and running well. Did I mention it only had 40,000 miles on it? I abandoned my idea that I had discovered the perfect buy. What I didn't pay for up-front, they certainly got from me on the back-end.

Be very cautious about how you represent your product's competition to your customer. Do not fall into the trap of bashing the competition as one of your primary sales strategies. You will find that you have hurt yourself more than helped.

Chapter 18

SAD STORIES

I cannot stand to read a major newspaper or turn on the evening news. It feels like one nightmarish story after another. I am the guy who doesn't even know a hurricane is bearing down on my home until the wind starts to blow. My friends bring up the latest gang violence, murder trial or bombing and they receive a blank stare. It is not that I don't care. The problem is that I do care and so I choose to keep it out of my life. The average Joe has enough anxiety, pressure and negativity to deflect in his average day without inviting other people's as well. Part of navigating this world is the continual effort we must make to lift each other up and focus on what's right most of the time. I am not trying to sound utopian, here. I recognize the need for dealing with bad things. I am simply stating that I, for one, refuse to go out of my way to experience more. Horrible things have been happening since the beginning of time. Go read the Old Testament. It is full of atrocities so violent and horrible, that even by today's standards, we cringe and cannot imagine what it must have been like. We just have better communication these days. We don't have to find a scribe to hand-write a letter about something and then wait centuries for it to become common knowledge. Within minutes, a message can go global with no more than a cell phone. Mankind has not gotten worse. We have just gotten far more efficient at sharing things with each other. And nothing hooks the public better than an awful spectacle. Consider the person who feels as though they have little else to talk about other than their ailments. We have all run into someone like this. That person is being the spectacle themselves. If the story is bad enough, you can't walk away. Even if you don't want to hear any more, you feel as though you are abandoning this poor person if you leave. So, you stay. In your living room, you keep the news rolling to do the right thing by the person suffering on the screen. You read that newspaper article to stay informed about who is suffering and where. It makes you feel more humanitarian to be aware, but when you do walk away, you feel worse about your world.

Mildred was a long-time TV shopper. She had the super-sharp knives, the pest repellers, the foot massager and a monthly delivery of various celebrity skin care products, among other things. She loved her purchases. She knew she had gotten great deals on products admired for their uniqueness. Her friends told her so. She felt truly connected to the hosts on her favorite channel. They kept her company as she went through her day. She had been watching long enough to know about their families, vacations and lifestyles. They felt like her friends and were always warm and kind.

As usual, Mildred had her TV on in the background as she made her coffee and fed Rufus, who purred thankfully and rubbed against her robed leg. There were times of the day that she desperately needed that companionship from Rufus and the uplifting conversation coming from her favorite shopping channel. It had been almost a year since she lost William. Forty-three years together and now she awoke each morning expecting to hear his shaver running in the hall bathroom and smell the coffee from the kitchen. Nothing. The house was silent, the coffee unmade until she pulled her robe on and went to hit the button. William had been such a gentleman, raised by a father who stood every time a woman entered the room and was always the last to enter the car, even in the rain. He woke 30 minutes before Mildred every morning to be sure that her coffee was ready and the bathroom was clean and available when she rose. She loved him so dearly. Following his death, her medication had to be increased. Her heart struggled more now than it ever. However, she did find solace in a few things. Rufus, her coffee, the chatter of her TV friends who were there every day without fail at the turn of a knob.

As Mildred walked by the shopping channel broadcast, she noticed the item being sold. A regenerator for non-rechargeable batteries. She had seen this item before and had wondered about buying it. She spent way too much money on batteries for the flameless candles in her windows. The device on the screen right now would bring those batteries back to life over and over again without having to buy rechargeables. Regardless of her fixed income, she decided to go for it. It should easily pay for itself in no time. She settled into her overstuffed chair, picked the phone up from the TV table on her right and dialed the number by heart.

"Thank you for calling. If you would like to purchase the current item, press 1. If you would like to purchase the previous item, press 2. If you would like to purchase a different item, press 3."

Mildred pressed one.

"Thank you for deciding to purchase the battery regenerator. Your credit card will be charged a total of $43.95. Please enter your account number to confirm your purchase."

Mildred punched the digits into the phone and listened for the response.

"Thank you. Your purchase is complete. Your item will be shipped today and should arrive within 7–10 business days. If you would like to purchase another item, press 1. If you would like to speak to our on-air host, press 2. To end your call, press 3 or simply hang up."

Mildred thought for a moment. Her heart was heavy this morning. She missed William so much. These shopping hosts had been her companions through many grey mornings. She would love to speak with one of them for real. She knew they would ask about her purchases and talk about the product she just bought. She certainly had a good reason for her purchase today and figured she might inspire someone else who could be having the same kind of morning. She pressed 2.

"Please stand by as we connect you."

A silence ensued and then an off-line producer answered. She was asked some questions about her account, information and nature of the testimonial she wished to give. She told the producer that she had about a dozen flameless candles in her windows and had been buying package after package of AA batteries to keep them going. The producer told her that she would be connected to the live show and to wait a few minutes. Mildred hung on the line and watched the action on screen. In a few minutes there was a "click" and a "Hello, Mildred. This is Liz here with Cory. I hear you bought our battery generator? Congratulations! Why did you decide to buy this today?"

Mildred looked up at the screen. Liz and Cory were looking right at the camera, right at her! Mildred began "Well, I have to buy a lot of batteries these days and I figure this'll save me some money."

"You bet it will! What do you use your batteries for, Mildred?"

Well, since my husband died about a year ago, I like to keep flameless candles lit around the house. It makes me feel like I have company. When they go on by themselves, it makes me feel like someone is there with me in the rooms. Besides, my heart isn't so good. I've had very high blood pressure and the doctors are talking about having to do surgery for a bypass pretty soon. I can't get back and forth to the store too often. It's just too hard on me. So, I figure this battery charger can help me."

"Ooooh, I'm so sorry to hear that, Mildred. I'm glad our regenerator can help you out. You have a wonderful day. Okay, bye-bye."

"Bye Bye, Liz," Mildred said.

The phone clicked to silence.

The host immediately turned to the product guest and asked him to once again go through the top reasons someone would want the battery regenerator.

Mildred hung up.

Although I have heard many stories much like this one, the story above is fictional and one I fabricated for the purpose of making a point.

Here is what things looked like behind the scenes at the shopping channel during our hypothetical scenario above: Right after Mildred mentioned the death of her husband, the producer began looking for a good opportunity to end the call. The host, producer and crew certainly felt sorry for Mildred, but the producer's job is to maximize airtime sales. The longer that call went on, the more the on-air host and producer were treading water. When she mentioned her heart trouble, the host had to be kind and gentle, but end the call ASAP. The producer's inner voice was hearing sirens and shouts of "Mayday! Mayday! We're going down!" Here's why. Every entertainer will tell you that from the first moment you walk on stage, you must let your audience know that you are in charge and feel great to be there with them. If you do not master them, they will master you. And if they perceive sadness or negativity, it will be your death publicly. It doesn't matter if your dog died, your girlfriend dumped you or your child is in the hospital. All that must drop away when you step in front of people. Why? Because emotions are contagious and if you are in the spotlight, your emotions can spread like unchecked wildfire. Once Mildred mentioned her woes, she was taking a positive, enthusiastic experience and turning it into a negative one for the entire nation, regardless of how much she deserved to talk about it. Other viewers began to sympathize with her. The host's natural reaction depressed the presentation and she knew she needed to turn things around quickly. People don't want to feel bad while making buying decisions. They want to feel great about laying out their money!

If they perceive sadness or negativity, it will be your death publicly.

If you have a personal story, a testimonial or a phone caller that spreads sadness, find a way to end that story as soon as you possibly can or cut it from your presentation plan. No matter how great it shows off the benefits of your product, it is not worth it. In the end, you will watch your sales slack off. There is a time and place for everything. A product presentation is not the venue for sorrow or suffering. Viewers will listen intently to the story, and then go hit the bathroom, get a drink, or tune out to do that other thing they just remembered. They know they are doing you a favor by watching. They will simply opt not to continue if you make it emotionally burdensome. Initially, they will do the right thing. They will listen to the story. They will sympathize and pacify their humanitarian side—right before they find a reason to walk away.

PUTTING IT ALL TOGETHER

Chapter 19

HOW TO GET THERE

Malcolm had just awakened in his hut. It was not on par with even the lowliest of American ghetto dwellings, but it was the best accommodation in the entire African village. The residents had insisted that he call it his home during his brief stay.

He swung his legs down onto the mud floor, and glanced around to be sure no unpleasant critters were lurking under the edge of his bed, ready to attack. His feet were still in his shoes. In a village this poor and remote, sanitation was completely foreign to the residents. There were many things mixed with the mud that could cause disease or infection. He was ever cautious.

He walked to the hut's doorway and glanced out at the village. It amazed him how people could live in such conditions. His heart screamed for them. He prayed each day for a radical change in their circumstances. Even the promise of fresh water or a septic system would be huge improvements. Yet this village will seem like Manhattan compared to where he is going. Today, Malcolm would traverse the Savannah to bring his message of love to those who had never seen a white man.

Following a breakfast of his own supplies, Malcolm loaded his pack and went to find his guide. Jabari, a Massai man with shaved head, hide sandals and red shawl around his lanky frame was heading toward Malcolm as he stepped out from under his grass roof. Jabari spoke broken English in addition to Swahili, his native tongue. He would not only serve as interpreter, but would walk Malcolm across the plains to his destination. It would take them three days. They would never even cross a road. It would be absolute wilderness. In all his years as a missionary, Malcolm had never traveled to a place so remote.

The journey began as anticipated. The companions neglected the rough road that acted as the thread connecting the Masaai village to civilization and headed toward the horizon of grasses, the wind creating infinite undulations across the sea-like expanse. Malcolm's mind was preoccupied with how he would be received by the people at his destination. He knew the customs of the region and the friendliness of its inhabitants, but he had never been to a place where he would appear so alien. And he was there to breach the chasm between himself and these people to explain the love of God. He prayed for guidance. He had no idea how to do what he was setting out to do.

As it neared ten in the morning, Jabari suddenly stopped Malcolm with an outstretched arm. Malcolm realized that he had spent most of the morning deep in thought, staring at the ground a few paces in front of him. He had not been taking in the landscape. They had just emerged from a grove of trees and in front of them, about 20 yards away, stood a herd of Elephants! Malcolm stopped breathing! He had never been so close to something so huge, so wild, so unpredictable! Malcolm looked around wondering how they could circumvent the herd and give them a wide berth. What met his eyes was stunning. He could not even tell where they had come from. There was no path. Every grove of trees looked the same, the grass plains stretching infinitely around them. He could turn to every direction of the compass and it looked the same. His guide carried no map, no compass, nothing to point his way. Even the sun was directly overhead and offered no point of reference. Malcolm's anxiety spiked. They were about to be trampled by charging Elephants as they ran in circles in an eternal, directionless wilderness.

"Jabari!" Malcolm spoke in a whisper charged with the raspiness of a shout. "Where are we? How do you know where we are going? Where is the path?" Jabiri turned to Malcolm with an inquisitive look. "The path, sir?"

"Yes! The path, the way, where is the way?" Malcolm stressed.

Jabiri leaned on his staff and his mouth widened into a smile showing the gap in his front teeth, the lines in his face creasing in amusement.

"Sir, I am the way."

This is a story from a South African missionary my father revered. I'm sure some of the details may be askew (I am recalling my father's rendition from my childhood), but the theme and message are accurate. If you are plunging into uncharted territory, trust your guide to know the way when you don't recognize it. Even if the path seems counter-intuitive.

I have vendors whose products I represent and who consult me daily on the politics, protocols and success tactics of television retail. I have been asked dozens of times to help guide new talent. I led a class at the network at one point, instructing fresh presenters on the nuances of on-air success. I also managed a crew helping new guests to understand the operations of a studio floor and prepared them to walk on air for the first time. As I explain what to focus on and what to negate, many new presenters push back. They had spent weeks thinking through how they were going to present their product and what I was telling them was not what they had constructed in their mind. They had elaborate stories they wanted to get to right away in their presentation, they wanted to explain the intricacies of the science behind their brand, they were convinced that their product would generate so much viewer enthusiasm that it would fly out the door with little salesmanship! They were wrong. Some of what they had imagined could be correct, given the right product, and presentation circumstances. But, for the most part, they were off-base. The horizon stretched endlessly, they had no compass and they had picked a direction, striding forward with resolve. The problem is that it was the wrong direction. The destination was closer than they thought. They just had to be open to a little course correction.

There are times when you can get from A to B with scribbled directions or a map. Other times, you need a GPS. Then there are the times when the only way to get where you want to go is through another person. You must be led and count on their knowledge and experience to get you there. Such is the case with a doctor or attorney. You do not lead. You follow their lead. My industry is not one with published manuals. You need to follow those who have blazed the path ahead of you. Sometimes, with the help of a strong guide, you need to partner and discover your own path. It might not be the same every time. It changes depending on the nature of your product and who you are selling to. However, there are some consistent rules that can help you discover the path to success. Follow my lead.

You need to follow those who have blazed the path ahead of you.

One of the best ways to discover your product's strongest attributes and the direction your presentation should take is by storyboarding. If you followed the advice of the former chapters, there are some basic questions you should have already answered in regard to your product. The answers to those questions will now point the way. Once the storyboard is completed, that is your guide. Follow it. Trust it. Share it with your sales staff. If your sales staff is your wife and kids, share it with them. Know it through and through so that every time you shake a hand and speak about your product, you know immediately how to resonate with your listener. It is your bible. Now, take up the path behind me and let's plunge into the Savanna together.

Chapter 20

THE STORYBOARD

I have outlined many elements to include and not include in your presentation. Now, let's take a look at a basic assembly of the important ones and how to bring them together into a formula that works. The storyboard is a living thing. It is fluid and can change dramatically, based on the nature of your product and demonstrations. So, I will insert a disclaimer here: The following statements and examples are meant to be an informational guideline. I am, by no means, guaranteeing universal success with this formula. When applying all the suggestions in this book along with your own intellect and product knowledge, your personal storyboard may take on a completely different variation. In most cases, some of the steps below may need to be omitted or repeated, as is necessary to do your product justice. However, with that said, the following is a good starting point for consideration. I will divide this chapter of the book into 2 parts. First, we will look at the structure of an internet video product presentation. Then we will consider a presentation for television retail.

The Internet Video Product Presentation (Shorter than Television by Design)

1. Product shot with name or logo superimposed (first 4–5 seconds)
2. Host (product presenter) delivers delivers the emotional appeal. This consists of a heart-felt relational statement of the problem the product fixes.
3. Host delivers Catch Phrase which should provide the solution to the former problem.
4. Host shows most impactful demonstration of product in action (When the demonstration speaks for itself, steps 3 and 4 can be done simultaneously to maximize time usage)
5. Host delivers top 3 "Key Points"
6. Brief testimonial or before/after (B/A) images (10–15 seconds, if applicable)
7. Host shows second most impactful demonstration or product usage/assembly (if applicable)
8. Second brief testimonial or B/A images (10–15 seconds, if applicable)
9. Host wrap-up and repeat of "Catch Phrase"
10. Closing product shot with name/logo (final 4–5 seconds)

The Television Retail Product Presentation

1. Host introduces product and goes through what the viewer will receive
2. Host covers pricing information and item number used to order
3. Host introduces guest (product presenter/expert)
4. Guest has a choice (depending on the product):
   a. Begin with the most gripping, hair-raising demo or B/A as they deliver the "Catch Phrase"
   b. Begin with the "Catch Phrase" while addressing the camera, product held in the shot if possible.
5. Guest now delivers the emotional appeal. This consists of a heart-felt relational statement of the problem the product fixes.
6. Guest delivers the statement of solution (the benefit the customer will receive and the product feature that delivers this benefit) at the same time as performing the second most impactful demo, (if applicable)

(Note: you should cover these first steps within your first 2–3 minutes on-air.)

7. Guest delivers the product's top 3 "Key Points" (while continuing demonstrations, if applicable)
8. Guest demonstrates how the product works or assembly (if applicable)
9. Host will now remind the viewer of the product's item number and pricing information as well as doing a Call-To-Action

10. Run Product testimonial and B/As (if applicable)
11. Host recaps product pricing and item number
12. Guest repeat's product "Catch Phrase"
13. Guest begins breaking down "Key Points" in more detail, focusing on benefits for the consumer (emotional appeal), then the feature that provides that benefit. (Continue demos, if applicable)
14. Host delivers pricing, item number and Call-To-Action
15. Guest delivers the emotional appeal, the statement of solution and the product "Catch Phrase"
16. Guest delivers top 3 "Key Points" in succession while repeating the most impactful demonstration or B/As (if applicable)
17. Host delivers Call-To-Action, pricing and item number
18. Host thanks guest and says goodbye.

You will notice that all the most impactful elements happen right at the top of each presentation. This is to capitalize on your viewer's attention. The idea is to keep your watcher watching! Even if they tune out after 30 seconds, they will have done so after seeing your product at its best. Think about a newspaper. What is the first thing you see at the top of a great story? Do they build suspense and make you wait for a big revelation later in the text? No way! They throw the biggest, juiciest, most revealing fact right into the headline! It's in 48-point, bold font at the top of the page! That's how they hook you. That's why you continue to read to find out what follows. Then, later in the story they give you all the support information, so you walk away feeling fully informed and satisfied. It is the same with a product presentation, with a little twist. At the end, you recap the most important reasons that your viewer was watching. You don't want them to walk away satisfied until they have bought your product. After you tell them the story, you want them to take action. So, after they hear all you have to say, you remind them what they should do next by recapping the benefit of buying your product. It is a subtle inspiration to pick up their phone or click the "BUY" button. You can only take them to third base, they must run home by themselves. You must thoroughly inspire them. In television retail, this actually happens several times throughout the presentation. The public channel-surfs. People tune in and out. You want to make sure the people who weren't watching right at the beginning of your presentation are grabbed by what they see and hear as well. Subtle repetition of your most impactful demos and statements ensures this.

Once again, let me stress that every product is different. I have scripted very successful presentations that start with a testimonial. Some products have no clear "Catch Phrase." It is more of a short story emotionally appealing directly to a common experience. Some products have started with a background demonstration behind the host who is introducing the product. Like I said before, a storyboard is living and fluid. You are the expert on your product. Use the previous presentation examples to help you brainstorm your own script. It is not as daunting and messy as you may think one you dive in and start assembling the pieces!

Activity

Most people will not do a thing until it is demanded of them. That is the reason for the call to action we discussed earlier. If you demand a decision, many people will make one. I am now demanding a decision from you. This is my call to action for you and your product. Take 30 minutes and roughly script your presentation based on the information in this chapter. It does not have to be perfect. Chances are, as you think about it throughout your day, you will probably come back to this outline and refine your ideas. But, you must start and now is the time while this chapter is fresh in your head. Of all the activities in this book, there are 2 that are most important: finding your key points and storyboarding. Without those two things, you do not have a direction or anything that can be called a presentation. Create the steps in your presentation now:

1. _____

2. _____

3. _____

4. _____

5. _____

6. _____

7. _____

8. _____

9. _____

10. _____

11. _____

12. _____

13. _____

14. _____

15. _____

16. _____

17. _____

18. _____

19. _____

20. _____

Chapter 21

SIZE MATTERS

At this moment in history, society is speeding up at an exponential rate, rapidly approaching frantic. In 1982, R. Buckminster Fuller, an inventor and futurist, estimated in his book *Critical Path* that if we looked at all the knowledge mankind accumulated since the beginning of time, it doubled between the year 1750 and 1900. By the end of World War II, it was doubling every 25 years. Currently, it is estimated to double every one to three years, depending on whose study you read. IBM predicted in 2006 that by 2010, the world's digital information base would double every 11 hours! Imagine what the numbers look like today.

The public consumes enormous amounts of information every day through wireless devices that deliver the cumulative knowledge of the known universe into their palm. In the world of Google, my teenagers cannot even conceive the use of a card catalogue. They cannot relate to wondering about anything for more than a few minutes without having the answer beamed to their phone. And those phones now sell for a dollar (with a 2 year contract, of course).

Friends, family and business associates now send a text or email and get frustrated if they do not hear back within a few minutes! The speed and efficiency at which business gets done, products get ordered and decisions get made is dizzying! In his book *Key Person of Influence*, author and entrepreneurial guru, Daniel Priestly, states that "Your best ideas from five years ago are your baggage today!" Just think, we need to reinvent our impressions of how business gets done and what ideas are viable every few years due to technology and what consumers expect!

In the wake of all this mental acceleration, the pace at which we move through our lives has sped up as well. We demand far more from ourselves. We talk faster and develop larger bases of friends (or Twitter followers) than we ever could have managed 20 years ago. We call or text each other from the master bedroom to the kitchen. It is faster than walking. Most gas stations offer us a three-minute car wash. Large stores offer self-checkout and cashiers don't handle change much in this world of swiping plastic. Billboards advertise attorneys for texting and driving accidents. People are typing, calling, surfing the web and social networking WHILE they are driving. If they didn't take the time during their commute, when would they keep up? We pack more into our days and expect others to manage their time the same as we do. We get upset if they move slower than us. And short of an apocalyptic event, it is not going to slow down—ever!

I already pointed out that 30% of viewers will click away from an online marketing video within the first 10 seconds. I have given you the tools to maximize your potential for continued viewership and marginalize the chances of losing those viewers. Those first 10 seconds are critical. However, as a whole, people (especially web browsers) do not have the attention span for long product sales videos. They want you to deliver the answers quickly or you will lose them.

Amazon.com asks for their product videos (or "Rich Media," in their lingo) to be 60 seconds in length. Many videos they currently have posted are longer than that, but 60 seconds seems to be their preference. They recognize that a video must deliver information quickly and with impact. Otherwise, the potential buyer will click away from the page. Longer videos are also larger files, making them more difficult to store on a server, upload or, email.

Shorter product videos offer more flexibility. They can grab people walking by a tradeshow booth without asking for a big time commitment. They can be used in television retail as support video for a product, on network television as commercials, incorporated into email marketing, posted on a product webpage or online marketplace. They can be added to a Vimeo.com or YouTube.com channel and referenced on social networking sites. They are simply more versatile, and they secure more completed viewings. If your product is a simple one (I would estimate, less than $200) and your video exceeds four minutes in length, you will lose viewers and limit your options.

Imagine, you are sitting at your desk dropping a quick hello to a friend. In the midst of your online activities, you run across a video for a product you could be interested in. You click "play." Right away, across the bottom of the video, the timeline pops up. Your eyes instinctively follow it to the right to check the overall time of the video. It says 11 minutes. What do you do? The dishes need to be washed, you need to make it to the bank, the kids are fighting in the next room, and you told your spouse a few minutes ago, "I'll be right there!" Do you watch the 11 minute video or click away? What if that video was three minutes in length? Would you be more likely to spare the time?

People want product information delivered quickly and in language that is easy to understand. They want something they can send as a link to their mother or son. Something that grabs them right away. Keep your videos shorter than longer. In this age of speed and efficiency, you must cater to the masses. You may have to omit what you believe to be important details, but in the long run, your simplifying will pay off and give you far more options and completed viewings! The next time Tom or Mary whizzes through cyberspace on their cell phone, give them the answers they need during their three-minute car wash. They will be more likely to click "order now" before the drying cycle spits them back into the fast lane.

Chapter 22

WHY YOU MUST HAVE AN INTERNET PRODUCT SALES VIDEO

Kevin could not believe his eyes. The man in front of him was using his kitchen knife to saw through the head of a hammer! He then used the same blade to slice transparently thin slices from a tomato! Kevin was amazed. He had been standing in the convention aisle for almost an hour, watching the presenter over and over again. Every single time he pulled out the hammer and then the tomato, a gasp went up from the crowd and hands reached for wallets. By the time his short 10 minute presentation was finished, more than half the people watching had bought a knife set.

Kevin was a smart guy. Raised by a hard-working father who passed on his ethic, Kevin had applied his unique mind to seeking out and solving common problems in uncommon ways. Currently, he was purchasing inexpensive overnight airtime on metropolitan TV stations to advertise franchise opportunities. He had been using classifieds in local newspapers, but discovered that TV networks did not have enough programming to fill the overnight hours, so the stations normally went black. By purchasing this airtime for relative pennies, Kevin had broadened his scope of potential readership by millions and was reaping the financial results of his vision with unprecedented success. However, as he stood in this convention aisle, his wheels began to turn.

Every time a crowd of 30 people gathered to watch this knife presenter, 15 people reached for their cash. What if the knife presenter could stand in front of 30 thousand people instead of 30? What if he could stand in front of a million? What if he did not need to even be present? What if he did his presentation once and then it got recycled over and over again day after day for years? The prospect ignited his ingenuity and the opportunity seemed too good to pass up. Kevin approached the knife presenter—and the rest is history. From that idea, we got the first infomercial. The Ginsu knife, shot in a grocery store produce department during overnight hours, became a household word. Its genesis was in the 80s, but even my kids, born 15 years later, know that product name.

I run my own <u>company</u> creating product sales videos for internet and television. I create lifestyle b-roll, which means I show a product being used in its natural environment outside of a studio. I also craft product demonstrations with voice-over for online marketing and full <u>Pitch Videos</u> (mini-infomercials) complete with a seasoned pitch host, model and branded environment. I specialize in items under $200 that offer simple solutions to homeowners. My company is streamlined for this exact purpose. I shoot no other type of video. A <u>Pitch Video</u> provides your best pitch and demonstrations without error every single time. It is the same concept as an infomercial. Do the work once to set everything up and then reap the results over and over again for years to come. This is what a product sales video or "<u>Pitch Video</u>" does. It represents your product in your absence. It allows you to provide your best pitch and demonstrations without error every single time a person is interested. It far outreaches your ability to be in a thousand places at once. It can be on television, on <u>Amazon.com</u>, in an email campaign, on your <u>YouTube.com</u> channel, on a TV screen at a convention and on your social networking sites all at once. Imagine standing in a trade-show convention selling your product in front of 50 people. Now imagine I have removed every other vendor in the tradeshow. Only you remain. Imagine I have elevated you and your demonstrations onto a stage in a spotlight and your voice is being broadcast through a sound system. Now imagine the 50 people in front of you have swelled to 50,000 and all of them have chosen to watch what you have to show them and listen to your words. That is the power of a good Pitch Video.

A <u>Pitch Video</u> provides your best
pitch and demonstrations without
error every single time.

Right now in 2014, within the next hour, in the US alone, 3.2 million people will watch an online video. Five years ago, this was not possible. The internet simply did not have the technology in place to handle that kind of demand. Now, the technology has caught up with what people want. It doesn't matter whether they are buying a car, a pair of shoes, a house or a brand of coffee. Consumers want to see a quick presentation making them feel emotionally confident in their purchase. With the advances in mobile technology over the past few years, video now accounts for more than 50% of all mobile traffic (source: Bytemobile Mobile Analytics Reports, 2013). Shoppers are now pulling up product videos in store aisles to help them make buying decisions. <u>Ice.com</u>, an online jewelry retailer, found that viewers who chose to view video converted at a 400% increase over those who didn't. The site also credited video with decreasing returns by 25%. It is a no-brainer. Anyone selling product online or otherwise who does not acquire demonstration video for their product will be left in the dust. They will have to wash the tire tracks from their backs after other vendors roll over them. They will stand on the station platform and watch the caboose disappear into the distance, loaded with those celebrating their vision in jumping on the video train.

Consumers want to see a quick
presentation making them feel
emotionally confident in their purchase.

Do your research. Look at the statistics. They are staggering. If you do not yet have video as a tool in selling your product, you are like the old lady who refuses to learn about cell phones. It is time to step up, or you will not be competitive much longer!

Activity

What is standing in the way of you having a compelling product video? List your reasons below:

1. _____

2. _____

3. _____

4. _____

5. _____

6. _____

If it was a priority to you, what resources could you tap to make it happen?

1. _____

2. _____

3. _____

4. _____

5. _____

If your marketing budget is re-appropriated to more effective, trending strategies, is that not the approach you should take? That's like free money when your sales increase!

Chapter 23

IS YOUR PRODUCT RIGHT FOR TELEVISION?

This is a question I am asked by more people than I can count. The current hit reality TV show Shark Tank is a testament to this. Thousands of inventors want the shot to get their product on TV. It is up to the "Sharks" (investors) to determine which ones are right for it and which ones are not. I have uncommon knowledge when it comes to this. I understand the process, what makes a product attractive to the TV viewer and which ones are destined to fail. Although this topic alone could be an entire book, I will do my best to provide a brief synopsis of what makes a product viable for DRTV (direct response television).

If a product does not sell, there can be a multitude of reasons why. There could be a big game or breaking news pulling people to a different channel at the time the product airs. It could be a holiday when everyone is out watching fireworks. The upper administration could have decided to cut or change their coverage area and no one down on the studio floor knows any better. The presenter could be the wrong one to resonate with the viewer on that product. The demonstrations could have failed to engage. The host could be poor at executing good CTAs. Perhaps the product lacks good support video, testimonials, before/afters, or another key element for the sale. The airtime could have been too short or too long. The product could be older technology. It could be on air too often, causing people to tire of seeing it. It could be the wrong season to air such a product. There are an almost indefinite number of factors to consider and it can be dizzying. This is why the merchandising departments for retail networks must be very discriminatory and plan carefully. They juggle all these reasons in their heads and attempt to make the best decisions when purchasing and planning products for air. However, there are some consistent factors that are non-negotiable when considering products for any kind of DRTV. At least one of these factors must be present for a product to be viable. If two of them are present, you could have a home run on your hands!

When a television retail viewer clicks the TV on and begins watching, she expects to see something she cannot find at her local store. They are expecting any of the following four things alone or in combination with each other:

1) Uncommon value
2) Uncommon functionality
3) Uncommon craftsmanship
4) Uncommon pricing or offer structure

Actually, the word "uncommon" might not be strong enough. Let's call it "surprising." It is never good enough to be just marginal with any of these characteristics. You must grab the viewer and you do not do that by giving them something slightly better than they can find elsewhere. Surprise your viewer! If your viewer can drive down to their local mart store and find a similar product of similar quality for a similar price, you cannot compete on TV. If they can have it in their hand that day without waiting a week for the mail or paying the cost of shipping, you will struggle and only sell to those few who are either ignorant, home-bound or simply don't care about money—a very small market indeed. So, the first thing you need to ask yourself is: "How is my product special?" Once you have answered that, we can look at the four characteristics above.

Surprise your viewer!

---

1. Uncommon Value

The very first thing a DRTV shopper looks for is pricing that knocks their socks off. They almost anticipate it. For the past 30 years, they have been hearing "But wait, there's more!" The entire genesis of television retail revolved around providing interesting products at awesome prices! When a product does not do well on TV, the product price is the first place all attention is focused. Producers, hosts, sales managers, directors, buyers and VPs all look at the price. Although this may or may not be the problem, it is the first consideration because it seems the most obvious culprit. So, let's talk price.

Television retail networks or infomercial companies set their profit margins based on the product category and sales history. Some are slightly higher or lower, but as a rule of thumb think half of the selling price. That means that if you plan to sell your product on TV for a price of $40 per item, you need to be able to manufacture it, package it, market it, pay your presenter, make your own profit and cover any other overhead expenses for around $20 per item. Right away, this eliminates many, many products. Television comes with a ton of expenses. It is not a cheap endeavor. Think of the expense of all the staff, buildings, equipment, air or satellite time. Heck, just the electric bill for most studios I have worked in is probably five times my annual income! Some of the larger television retail networks in this country employ thousands of people to make all that magic happen! Due to this, it takes a big chunk of the selling price to cover all those expenses and make a decent profit. Unless you are shooting your own infomercial with your own crew, booking the airtime personally and cutting out everyone else, you need to plan on providing your product for about half of what it will sell for, and your final selling price must be competitive.

2. Uncommon Functionality

I sell an air purifier that comes with a HEPA-type filter that never needs to be replaced. You vacuum it out and put it right back into the unit. It has a VOC filter that removes harmful chemicals from the air in your home. It also has a hospital-grade UV light, proven to kill airborne germs and bacteria. It is not your average purifier.

I sell a mosquito trap that does not use any chemical baits, shock screens, open flames or propane tanks. It works indefinitely with no maintenance (other than emptying the bug carcasses) and it will attract mosquitoes from up to an acre around it.

I sell an LCD door viewer that allows its user to see the person knocking on a big color LCD screen and it mounts over the peephole the user already has. She can press the power button, illuminating the screen 1,800 times on one set of AAA batteries.

I sell a portable lantern that uses an internal dynamo and a hand crank to provide its power. 60 seconds of easy cranking will give you 30 minutes of super-bright light before it even begins to dim. It also converts from a lantern to a focused spotlight with the push of a button and will even charge your cell phone. The user never buys another battery for his flashlight and knows he will always have light when he needs it.

You get the picture. When people tune in to DRTV, they are riveted by products that address common problems in uncommon ways. It does not matter if it is a dress that makes you look slimmer, cookware that makes molten marshmallow slide around on its non-stick or a hose that self-recoils. The viewer wants to see something that gives them an "Aha!" moment. They want excitement at the prospect of getting that product home and watching it do its magic! They want to show it to others who will ogle over it and pat them on the back. They want it to be easy to set up and simple to use. They want it to solve a problem in a way that other products cannot. Most of all, they want their lives to be easier, better and more convenient. This is a foundational concept for all DRTV. It is the reason it is a multi-multi-billion dollar empire.

3. Uncommon Craftsmanship

I have a buddy who sells solar lights. Not just any solar lights. Solar lights with the largest, most energy efficient LEDs on the market. The light housings are constructed of stainless steel with thick, real glass lenses. The lawn spikes are made of solid aluminum. The solar panels are twice the size of most other brands. They will run continuously with brilliant light for 12 hours on a single charge and their styling is gorgeous! They are the highest quality I have ever seen and although the price is slightly higher than most people would consider for solar lights, they sell like hot cakes. Why? Because people are familiar with the cheap plastic, dim, yellowed-lens lights that turn on for an hour and then die. They bought them at their local home improvement store and then disposed of them after 1 season in their yard. My buddy's lights leave others in the dirt!

I sell a tiny action camera that costs more than $400. Why would someone buy a compact video camera for $400 when they have one on their cell phone? Because mine is made to withstand a drop onto concrete from 10 feet. It can be left in the snow, and then plunged down 197 feet underwater. If it was constructed any better, it would deflect bullets. It can mount to the top of a surfboard, a helmet, the hood of a car, the underside of a skateboard or an airplane wing—*and* it shoots ultra-HD, cinema-quality video! It has been used by major movie houses to gather unique shots that no other camera can get.

I have sold bladeless fans and vacuums for Dyson. When people buy one of those products, they are buying superior quality, technology, appearance and a unique overall experience. You are not getting a disposable item. You are buying an item meticulously designed to last, to outperform any competition and look beautiful doing it. For this, people are willing to pay a premium price.

The quality your item can boast has much to do with how much people are willing to pay. However, be warned. There are many products that claim quality and do not have it. Your customer is aware of this and very skeptical. You cannot just claim your product is made better; you must be able to show it in ways that set it apart. Companies like Apple, Dyson and Lancôme have reputations for outstanding quality, but most products do not. Unless you have big time brand recognition, you must be able to drop or submerge your video camera, or disassemble your solar light to show the steel and glass. To claim manufacturing quality and make it believable, you must have an irrefutable way to substantiate that claim.

4. Uncommon Pricing or Offer Structure

This last characteristic is one used very effectively by most live retail TV networks and allows the customer convenience when it comes to payment. Unfortunately, the vendor has no real control over whether the network will decide to make this part of the product offer or not. It is one of the network's tools, to use at their own discretion to inspire customers that might be on the fence. Instead of paying $200 for a cookware set, the network will break up the payments into 4 equal installments of $50 per month charged to a major credit card. In the meantime, they send the cookware set to the customer to use, even though full payment has not yet been made. I have seen very expensive offers do incredible sales based on this element alone. If the item is desirable and popular enough to the masses, it can fly off the shelves when pricing makes it accessible to the person who could not normally afford to pay for it all at once. Notice that I said "popular and desirable enough to the masses." We're talking about the iPad here, not some unknown can-opener.

Another way to appeal to the customer is through the offer itself. In this, the vendor has more control. If you can offer a package that includes several items for one price, negating the customers need to accessorize or shop around afterward, you could inspire viewers to buy even though the selling price is just average. This is the least impactful way to ensure DRTV sales and is almost always presented with some form of pricing initiative like the one mentioned above. However, depending on your product, it can be worth considering.

There are many other tools used to inspire sales, such as "buy one, get one free," reduced shipping costs or "free set-up in your home by a professional" offers. However, they are superfluous to the major four I have listed above. They help, but are not a basis for DRTV success. The merchant who considers your product will also be looking for product support elements like high quality lifestyle b-roll (showing your product being used outside the studio in its natural environment), a good presenter, celebrity or professional endorsements, third party studies, great demonstrations proven to work and a solid sales record that shows promise. They want fast manufacturing times and the ability to provide a large inventory (hundreds or thousands at a time, depending on your product). In live retail television, the merchant will be looking for the next item you can offer if your first is a success. They appreciate product lines, variations and up-sells, not just single products.

My phone rings daily with questions from vendors about such topics. They all want the inside scoop. This could also be another book. But, at the end of the day, it all comes down to basics: Can you provide an uncommon offer that makes a good profit and helps to elevate the status of the network or invested company?

Look at the four main sales characteristics above. Measure your product against them and decide if you have what it takes. If DRTV is your goal, this brief analysis will give you a good indication of your potential success!

Activity

Scan the following QR code:

Or go to "www.pitchvideo.com/test and provide your email for access to an online test that will measure your product's viability for television sales!

Chapter 24

HOW TO GET 2,000,000,000 YOUTUBE VIEWS

Everything was ready to go. I had arrived early to make sure the game system was set up properly, long before my airing time. I now walked back into the studio knowing that everything had been tested and was working flawlessly. I changed into a more presentable shirt, ducked into the makeup salon to get powder dusted on my face and was now ready for my presentation. Since the item following mine was a large plasma TV, I had been positioned in area three of studio C. The TV was scheduled to air there after me. It was supposed that if I sold my game system utilizing the TV, viewers might like the TV as well and order early on that item. Normally, I sell this product in area two, which provides lots of space to move around, and since my item was the Wii moving around was important. Area three is restrictive, not offering the same kind of space as area two. However, I agreed to make do, knowing that the strategy was a solid one and willing to help out in any way I could.

As I approached the set, the cameras had all been positioned in a semi-circle around area three, obscuring my view of the table containing my game system and the TV. I could see a few people moving around in front of the table, but could not make out what they were doing. This made me a bit nervous. Usually, when things were set and ready to go, no one fooled around with them. But now, people were there. I was pulled aside by the stage manager for a microphone and IFB (the tiny speaker in my ear) check, and then asked to get into position. The host was running from one studio to another during a commercial break between items and would be joining me in about five minutes. As I rounded the cameras, I noticed the backstage crew was struggling to get the Wii remote to operate. It kept losing connection with the console, a warning jumping up and down off the screen, telling the user that the connection had been lost. This was an easy one. I had seen it many times. The remote batteries were dying. I told the crew as much and asked for a fresh set of AA batteries. They glanced at the countdown clock, seeing that they now had less than 3 minutes to get everything ready to go and dashed out of the studio. Batteries were kept in the backstage coordinator's prep area, about 100 yards away. It was where everything going to air is prepared, tested and propped out. Fresh batteries are supposed to be put into all products before going to air, so they do not run low during a presentation. This dead Wii remote was a ball that was dropped. It happens, but rarely. The backstage crew is very good at their job.

As they were running back onto the set, batteries in hand, the clock read less than a minute until we went to air. The host had now joined us and was doing a last-minute touchup of hair and make-up in a hand-held mirror before greeting the live viewers.

The game I had chosen to start my demonstrations with was tennis, one of my absolute favorites when playing the Wii. The product configuration we were selling came with some accessories for several of the Wii Sports games—a baseball bat, a golf club and yes, my racket. They attached to the remote using a cradle into which the remote was placed. The accessory then snapped onto the outside of the cradle. However, to get new batteries into the remote, you had to unsnap the racket and pull the remote out of the cradle. With the clock ticking down, the crew was trying to short-cut the process by keeping the remote in is cradle while wedging the battery cover open and cramming the new batteries down under the cover. It wasn't working. In my IFB, I can hear the director counting us down until we go live. "Cory, we are coming to you in 20 seconds...15...10,9,8,7..." I ripped the remote out of the backstage coordinator's hand, snapped off the remote, pulled the remote from its cradle, inserted the new batteries, slammed in back into its cradle and re-attached the tennis racket accessory. The camera tally light clicked on just as the racket slid into place on the remote and I swung my arm to begin playing.

What I noticed in retrospect was that the familiar "click" sound telling me that the racket was fully in place never happened. Apparently, the battery cover was still a bit askew, the remote was not lying fully in its cradle and therefore, the racket could not snap fully into place. Have I mentioned that I play tennis? I love the game and I have a hell of a serve. I really get into Wii tennis and I play all-out.

About half way through my presentation, I was describing how accurately the Wii mirrors the motion of the remote. As a demonstration, I brought my racket up to serve and my arm swung down like I was at Wimbledon. Because of the restrictive dimensions of area 3, I was playing far closer to the TV than I normally would—awkwardly close. Somewhere in the arc of my serve, the loosely attached racket sought freedom. It happened in a blink. The racket flew from my hand, hit the plasma TV, shattered the screen and ricocheted off, flew under the leaping feet of the stage manager and came to rest in the hallway outside of the studio, about 40 feet away. Did I mention I have a strong serve? I've wounded friends of mine with it!

The following moments were interesting ones. The director immediately went to a pre-recorded b-roll (tape with no audio) of game play while I spoke over it. My host became completely useless. She walked over to a nearby wall and leaned against it, laughing hysterically. The studio crew was in shock, and then completely lost all composure, joining my host. These are the moments that define your career. The nation is watching. I just smashed a 60" plasma screen on live television and the show must go on. I continued to sell, encouraging people to "make sure their accessories are latched on all the way," and admitting that I had failed to do so. I then looked into the camera lens, knowing my director and producer were watching and shrugged as I was talking. My producer said into my IFB, "Uuuh, Cory, I can't come back to you and show that TV. It's destroyed." I began shifting my body side to side in front of the smashed plasma screen. He understood. "Ok, Cory, take a baby step to your left. Right there! Ok. Coming back to you." The camera tally light winked to life and the nation was watching again, but now, my body was blocking the huge smashed part of the screen behind me. My host rejoined me and we continued to sell the Wii. Six minutes later, we sold it out. Six hundred Wiis sold, 300 of them after I smashed the TV.

If I had ever known how much press that one mistake was going to make, I would have asked the network to let me smash a TV on air long ago. Within an hour, it was on YouTube.com. By the next morning, I was front page news on AOL and Yahoo. CNN and MSNBC covered the story. Keith Olbermann made it part of his top ten list and the local morning show was raving about it as I drove to work. By the following week, some creative person had made an online music video with it, showing me smashing the TV over and over. It was unbelievable! And I went on to sell tens of thousands of Wii game systems on national TV.

Half of the public was veracious and ugly in their online comments. Half were understanding and complimentary in how I handled it. Either way, it didn't matter. People are ravenous for something of significance to hitch their wagon to, good or bad. It never fazed me. This incident actually acted as a springboard for my career. The upper ranks of the network were complimentary of my professionalism, improvisational skills and ability to keep the sales rolling in regardless of the disaster that came out of nowhere! I was told that "I really shined that day." It is not just in your successes that you have an opportunity to impress people. It can be far more impressive when others see how you handle a disaster! But, that is another book entirely, geared toward aspiring talent.

This I do know. The public loves "Infotainment" more than information. Comedic videos get passed around on social networking sites and they get forwarded in emails and texts. They go viral. I am not insinuating that you should go out and smash a TV or be comedic at the expense of your product. However, there is some truth to the value of a genuine blooper! If you capture any footage of your product in action and things go awry, make it public (as long as it was user error)! That one ten-second clip could prove to be your greatest unexpected blessing! Although, you may have to live with prods from your friends who feign fear and tell you please not to attack them with a Wii remote!

Chapter 25

ME, IN A VERY
SMALL BOX

I fixed my first small engine at the age of 12. It was the first of my enterprises that did not include my parent's wallet. A neighbor was throwing an old lawn mower away. I took it from the curb, pulled the engine apart, cleaned it out, replaced a few gaskets and got it running. I was always good with tools and fixing things. I then went from door to door asking people if they wanted their lawn mowed. Within a few weeks, I had seven lawns. I charged between three and eight dollars for a yard in my neighborhood. It was not a fortune, but at age 12, in 1985, I had a steady summertime income when all of my friends were stuck with allowances.

Over the next few years, I did two paper routes, shoveled snow, raked leaves, walked dogs and washed cars, all before the age of 14. At that age, I went to work at an old car lot and painted the buildings. It was eight miles from my home through rolling Pennsylvania farmland. I rode my bike back and forth each weekend. To this day, I hate to paint, but I'm good at it. At 15, I was hired by my best friend, Dean, to mow lawns. He had about 30 lawns, a truck (he was 16 and driving), a trailer and equipment for two people. Within two years, Dean and I were mowing 67 lawns a week and working 6am to 6pm, five to six days a week. During the winter months, I worked as a handyman at a local garden center, a janitor at a nursing home and a coal-bagger for a local distributer. Anything I could do to have an income, so I didn't have to wear the hand-me-downs from my older brother Jeff.

My family lived in an old farmhouse. The farmland itself had been mostly sold over the century since the house was built, but the barn and 11 acres (out of thousands) remained. Needless to say, my skills with tools came in handy. I rewired our barn, converted the old stalls into a workshop, built furniture, installed windows and did other general modifications to the property.

While Dean and I were mowing together, I turned 16 and got my first vehicle, a 1964 Ford pickup I paid $400 for. In Pennsylvania, vehicles require an annual inspection. My truck failed most of it. I can still remember the words of the guy who slapped the "approved" sticker on the truck's window. "If anybody asks where you got this sticker, you have no idea. Your brakes are almost shot, the play in your steering is way beyond the legal limit, you're burning more oil than gas and your wheels could fall off and the front end of your truck could drop and hit the road at any moment. I am only passing you because you are going to promise me to fix all these things ASAP." In that moment, I was handed my freedom! That truck did not land me a girlfriend, but it sure did develop my character! And I paid for it and fixed it myself with lawn-mowing money.

Since then, I have owned 20 vehicles—other Fords, Chevys, VWs, Jeeps, Toyotas, Lincolns, BMWs, Hondas. I'm like a walking consumer reports on car brands and I have fixed most of their minor problems myself.

After leaving home to head for college in Florida, I ran my own lawn/landscaping business, repaired all the engines myself when problems would arise. I then became a wedding DJ. I had run a small DJ service with some buddies of mine in high school. We bought some old band equipment, printed our own business cards in our high school graphics arts class and then ran around in my truck doing school dances. It was fun and a fast lane to local popularity. We loved it. Since then, I have done over 180 wedding receptions and have watched brides fall to pieces over and over because the color of the napkins was off or the floral arrangements were delivered 20 minutes late. In later years, I would tell Elizabeth, when we planned our wedding, I wanted things to be absolutely stress-free and simple. She agreed completely. An hour before our wedding, we were jumping on the trampoline with my brothers and sisters in my family's front yard. Elizabeth and I looked at a watch and said "Hey, we better get ready! We're getting married in 45 minutes!" It was awesome! We were married in bare feet by torchlight surrounded by wildflowers on the family farm's back porch. But, I am getting ahead of myself.

After getting tired of lugging DJ gear around, I became a cruise ship DJ. I was quickly promoted to club manager, cruise director and finally, corporate director of entertainment. I designed, built and maintained night clubs and show lounges with huge audio and lighting systems. I managed all the bands, DJs, cruise directors and entertainers. I was also the guy who would walk out on stage with a wireless microphone and improvise games and entertainment for cruise passengers waiting for the onboard casino to open. I hosted karaoke, bingo and skeet shooting. I was the guy with pockets full of free drink tickets and a witty remark was there to keep everyone happy on their cruise. On weekends, while not at sea, I worked in big night clubs (2,000+ people) as a DJ and for a time, I was broadcast live on a top 40 station as the DJ for their Friday night dance party. I never embraced the night club lifestyle, but loved the art of DJing. That was back when DJs still played everything on records and I would continually layer up to 3 songs simultaneously to create custom mixes. The first time I watched a guest DJ walk into a club with a laptop and a scratch record, I knew the art of DJing was about to die. I didn't have long to wait. Within three years, turntables were relics and computers were self-mixing the songs on night club dance floors. I stepped down from DJ work in January, 2004, after a shooting in one of the clubs where I worked. Two bouncers were shot right in front of me and the shooter ran into the DJ booth to hide the gun. One of those bouncers would later die in critical care. I sold every record I owned, nearly 3,000 of them, for a quarter a piece. It was very painful. It took me 12 years to build that collection, but I knew as long as I owned them I would be tempted to go back to DJ work. It pays well if you're decent at the job and it's always cash, but the environment was not one I wanted to have as a part of my regular lifestyle any more.

During the time I was working all these jobs, many of them at the same time, I was going to college. Because of my workload, it took me 7 years to get my bachelor's degree, but I finally graduated with honors in 1999 at age 26. I was the first person in three generations of my family to finish his degree. I decided to pursue my life-long dream of hiking the Appalachian Trail from Georgia to Maine, 2,200 miles in five months. I had no career, no marriage, no mortgage—the timing was perfect. I prepared for that hike for a year, sold everything I owned, put the rest in storage and reduced my entire life to a backpack. I have had a life-long love affair with the mountains and nature. It was common for me, as a teenager, to disappear into the Pennsylvania Appalachians for days at a time. I love to hike. I adore the sound of wind in the trees, the smell of the forest and the solitude. I have craved it my entire life. When I started preparing for my big hike, I did not foresee the curve-ball life would throw me next! As a result, my hike lasted only 8 days and stretched 100 miles. Then, I returned home and used my savings on a ring.

I was 27 and had fallen hard for a girl I met several years previously while DJing on the cruise ship. She and I had 1 date after our initial meeting. Then she left town, got married, had two children, got divorced and moved back again. Five years after our first date, she happened to walk into the night club where I was working. (Trying to cram that story into two sentences does it no justice at all. But, this book is not about that story. If I were to tell it in full, it would require its own binding.) Eighteen months later, following 100 miles in the Georgia mountains, I was ready to become a father and a husband to this woman I loved. We were married in August of 2000 and I had an instant family, a wife and two children, ages three and five. That was one of the hardest times of my life demanding more of me than anything ever had. I had aspired to become a film director, but that world is full of starving freelancers trying to scrape together enough money for their next meal while making a name for themselves. It was not very conducive to family life. So, I changed my focus to television. Just outside of my family's town resided one of the largest retail television networks in the US. I needed a dependable job with good benefits for my new family and that network had some openings.

I started there as a backstage coordinator. My job was to check out all the products before they went to air and then display them prettily for the camera. Always hungry for new experience, I quickly moved to audio operator and began cross-training myself on other positions during my lunch breaks or any other spare moments I could find. Soon, I was covering shifts as a camera operator, stage manager, graphics operator and director. When a director position became available, I was a shoe-in. I worked my way into prime-time and remained in that job for a year until I was promoted to Control Room Supervisor. In that position, I managed my own crew and was ultimately responsible for the technical execution and aesthetics of the daily broadcast. During those years, many of the network hosts grew to know me well from our daily work together. Several of them began pushing me toward on-air talent work, telling me I had everything it takes. Many DRTV show hosts were my proactive mentors, encouraging me toward the other side of the lens. In 2004, after a long campaign with the talent department, I got my first audition. I had to sell a gold watch and an Elvis telephone to a camera for five minutes. I was loaded with confidence. I had no doubt that I would knock their socks off! Afterward, I was told that I was among the best auditions they had ever seen, but I looked like a teenager in his dad's jacket. I was 31, I looked 21, but they wanted me to look 41! National networks have an image and I have always had a young face. Apparently, that's a blessing and a curse.

Shortly after that audition, my wife, Elizabeth, asked if I would be willing to step down from my career in television to become a stay-at-home dad while she pursued her dream of supporting us as a professional singer. Elizabeth's voice is one that when you hear it, you wonder how she wasn't snatched up by a record company long ago. If I were to outline her resume, experience and networking skills, you would see very quickly that it is only children and family that have kept her from stardom. She has been on the fast track several times in her life and has stepped away, choosing her family instead. Now, she wanted to give it another shot with my support.

In late 2004, we moved to Nashville and she began working her magic. It was not long before she was hanging with big-time record executives, famous songwriters and artists. I was at home with four children, ages eleven, nine, two and four months. I had never worked so hard in my life. At first, I spent all day in the kitchen preparing meals that the dog wouldn't even eat. The kids sat around the table frowning down at their plates silently. I would saw through my chicken, muscle down a bite, then say, "Okay, guys, get your jackets. We're going out." A year later, I could throw open a sparse pantry, invent a delectable dinner in 30 minutes and have the kids asking for seconds! Funny enough, the big country hit "Mr. Mom" by Lonestar had just topped the charts and living in Nashville, I heard it over and over again every day.

> "Pampers melt in a Maytag dryer
> Crayons go up one drawer higher
> Rewind Barney for the eighteenth time
> Breakfast six, naps at nine
> There's bubble gum in the baby's hair
> Sweet potatoes in my lazy chair
> Been crazy all day long and it's only Monday
> Mr. Mom"

The lyrics were precise to my life.

We were in Nashville for 18 months. During that time, Elizabeth became disenchanted with the politics of the music industry and her father's business in Tampa began having some real trouble. The kids were missing their grandparents terribly and Elizabeth's sponsor came on rough financial times. We decided to move back home to Tampa.

The television retail network had given me an open door if I ever wanted to return. So in late 2006, I returned as a freelance director, camera operator, stage manager and audio operator, which basically amounted to filling in for vacation coverage throughout the entire production crew. At the same time, I received word that the network was holding guest auditions. There are usually two people on the air at any given time. The host, who is the face of the network and leads the viewer through two to three hours of products, and the guest, who is an expert on just the one product that happens to be on air at that moment. Within an hour, one host will typically work with 3–5 guests who move on and off the air with their products. The exception to this is when the guest has their own line of jewelry, cosmetics or fashion items. In that case, the guest will remain on air for the presentation of their entire product line. Needless to say, a guest is someone who needs to build the number of products they represent over time. They are not handed a contract guaranteeing them a salary. Guests are generally paid by the vendor who provides products to the network. I auditioned for the role of guest. They loved me! It took a few months, but slowly, I began to get referrals from network buyers and product vendors, calling me to represent their products. However, it took three years before I could support my family on my income with guesting work alone.

During that time, I continued to freelance in the network's production crew and work in their wood shop as a carpenter, building studio furniture, set walls and props. I built beautiful things out of wood, my life-long hobby. I have also owned four homes and have done all my own remodeling work, from framing to electrical work, duct work, tile work, plumbing, cabinetry, dry-walling, painting and texturing, you name it. At one point, I was even offered a job by a general contractor for my skills and attention to detail! One day, a buddy of mine who ran the network's wood shop called me. He needed help the following day. I agreed and by the end of the next day, the foreman offered me a freelance position. It was common for me to show up at 8am at the wood shop, work as a carpenter until noon, shower off at a local gym, change into nice clothes, go on-air in the afternoon, then change my shirt and walk straight into the director's chair. What a juggling act! But, it provided for my family as I nurtured my on-air career.

Ultimately, I loved being on-air. I was able to reach out to millions of people and offer them awesome solutions to common problems. I got to reach into my experience and give my viewers insight they might otherwise not have had. I was able to help them fix things, avoid problems and educate them on how things work. I always thought I would make a dynamic teacher. I now had the chance to do exactly that, but with a classroom of tens of millions! With my experience on the backside of a camera, I was able to offer my vendors insight into what could and could not be accomplished on-air, a rare commodity. In the decades long history of that network, I am one of only two people to go from the production crew to on-air work. The other person is a former producer, who currently works as a guest in the "Home Solutions" category, but even he was not involved in the technical execution of the program. He relied on his directors, cameramen and technicians for that. He relied on me.

Since then, I have represented items at other shopping networks outside of the US, hosted infomercials and internet marketing campaigns, and have been the face of major brands such as Disney, Brighthouse, Karcher and others.

My story is a long one and the text above does it no justice. No year or even month of my life has been without its own distinct adventures. It is the way I live. There are always vivid memories of the last thing, the excitement of the moment and the anticipation of the next thing. As I sit here writing, I can reflect on last month's 40-mile trek through the Appalachians, the new business I am developing daily and my wife's beach concert I am preparing for. I've found the perfect spouse. Elizabeth is the same as me. Loving mother, professional singer, EMT firefighter and founder of her own ministry here in Tampa and all the way to Cuba. She is a dynamic woman. Nothing is ever boring around the Bergerons. It has made for quite a story, which leads me to the next big point in this book.

Chapter 26

BE AUTHENTIC

A few years ago, I was presenting wind spinners during a network lawn and garden show. I had come in early to be sure the spinners were displayed properly. When the time came to present my item, I stepped on-air knowing they would sell like hotcakes. The price was awesome, the spinners high-quality and attractive. I knew every step of the sell and had knocked that presentation out of the park a hundred times over the years. It went very well. As the presentation wrapped up, I took my cue to step off to the side and hand things off to the next presenter. As I stepped to my right to walk off set, the host said, "...and Cory will be sticking around with us for our next few items!" My foot never hit the ground. I swung my leg around in an arc and planted it right back beside my host again. The wind spinners had been removed from the table and something else was going to be put there. I had no idea what it was.

Apparently, there had been a communication breakdown somewhere and I was never contacted about presenting other items nor given any specifics as to what they were! When you are part of a 24/7 juggling act with thousands of products moving in and out of people's emails and offices, every once in a while, something slips through the cracks.

The backstage crew walked out with some large planters. There were 4 different styles and colors. I had about 30 seconds to plumb my experiences and memory for reasons these planters would be attractive to our demographic before the host was going to turn to me and say, "So, Cory, tell us why these planters are so great!"

As the backstage crew was carrying the planters, I noticed they seemed light, even though they were very large. As soon as the crew put the planters down, I ran my hand along the interior to confirm my suspicion. Yup, they were made of resin. I could feel the telltale fibers just under the smooth exterior lip. That meant they would not discolor or crack. They were light weight and durable. The pots also had a raised bottom with a tray, keeping the soil and roots above any standing water, so they would not rot from overwatering. When the host turned to me with the anticipated question, I said "These are the pots that will last you years without cracking or fading from weather. You can move your plants indoors and back outdoors as you please, because they are lightweight. No more pottery that cracks, weighs a ton and is a permanent fixture. And anyone looking would have to put their head inside the pot to know there was a difference. They look like real ceramic!" I proceeded to pick up each huge pot with one hand and hold it like a waiter's tray as I described why you were less likely to kill your plants with overwatering using these pots. We sold them out in one airing. I continued to use the same tactic with each of the next three lawn and garden items which included chaise lounges, lawn ornaments and fountains. Each one sold according my own life and gleaned knowledge. Needless to say, I was far more prepared the next time I aired those items, but my experiences were my saving grace. Without my background, I would have been lost. Without my background, I would have had no business being on national television selling lawn/garden products!

Why have I outlined all of this for you? Because it emphasizes my final point in creating a great product presentation. What you have read in these last pages is where I come from. It is the super-condensed CliffsNotes of a long adventure with many twists and tales, most yet untold. It is what has shaped my abilities and skills. It is the lens through which I interpret my world. It is what empowers me to speak with authority within specific categories of products. When people ask, I am likely to have the answer or some unconsidered insight. I am the genuine article, not some hyped-up poser struggling to relate to their customer.

Your viewer is sharp and has BS radar that is very acute. If you do not speak to them with authenticity and from within your own experience, they will know and your sales will suffer. I am fortunate. I have always craved knowledge, adventure, and experience. I respect the power of words and those who can wield potent language. I have an analytical mind that loves to take things apart, fix them and put them back together. I also have a big heart and have always been passionately engaged with my family. There are many, many products that I can represent and fit nicely within my experience and passions. However, not everything does. I would never represent a clothing line, a line of perfumes or jewelry. I have no expertise in these realms. However, if you want me to show off a backpack, toy, vacuum, pressure washer, wrench set, camcorder, cookware or doormat, I'm your guy! If it makes sense coming from a DIY'er, Mr. Fix-it, MR. Mom, or from a guy who could build you a house, a china cabinet, a concert audio system or a television studio, I'm who you want. I can speak as a man who learned early how to work hard, the value of a dollar and how to make it last. I understand the psychology of a parent, of a child and of Middle America. I know how to keep a house, raise children, keep the cars running and build custom bunk beds. I am the culmination of so many specific influences, as are you.

I am, therefore, going to leave you with this last nugget of hard-earned wisdom: You need to speak from these same places when you are selling a product. Whether you are writing your storyboard for an online video, coaching your talent or preparing to walk into the spotlight yourself, your own story is your most valuable and compelling tool. You cannot fool your audience. Don't try. Your credibility is everything. Speak with authenticity. Speak from within your own deep experiences and heart. Speak from what you thoroughly know. Your viewer is far more likely to believe you, trust you and buy from you!

LAST WORD

Relationship is important to me. In my faith, my career and my personal life, relationship has always been at the epicenter. Thank you for reading these pages. I hope that within them you have found wisdom and perspective to help you sell your product.

I want to continue this relationship with you. Selling a product is not a finite pursuit. It is a journey with many obstacles, times of feast and times of famine. I have created a company to walk that path with you and support you. You can, of course, find me on Facebook, Twitter and Google+. You can also go to PitchVideo.com where my regular blog and instructional videos are posted, all of which are free for you to peruse. Stop by and stay connected with the latest insights from the retail television studio front lines.

See you on the other side of the lens!

Cory

ABOUT THE AUTHOR

Cory Bergeron is best known to television audiences as DRTV's all-American "Dad," a family man and expert on household solutions and electronics. In the past five years alone, Cory has personally presented over 200 products on television and has grossed over $100,000,000 in sales. For 20 years, Cory has also been entertaining on stages, through talk radio and live television, commercials and infomercials.

In addition to his extensive talent resume', Cory has decades of experience in audio and video production. Having had great success as a videographer, audio engineer, stage manager, director and producer, Cory understands what can be accomplished on both sides of a lens, making him a valuable and rare asset to many companies. In a corporate environment, Cory has both directed and produced videos for some of the largest corporate giants in America, including Canon USA, Alcon pharmaceuticals, Motorola, Dunkin Doughnuts, Goodyear, Xerox and many others.

Cory is the founder and president of Pitch Video, a company that creates custom product sales videos for internet and television. Pitch Video is Cory's way of bringing all his talents and experience to a single table for the benefit of his client.

Cory is a proud husband and father of four. He and his family reside in Tampa, Florida.

CPSIA information can be obtained
at www.ICGtesting.com
Printed in the USA
JSHW041508141222
34891JS00001B/59

9 781630 471309